Frankfort
A PICTORIAL HISTORY

Houseboats have always been a popular form of recreation for Frankfort residents. Harry A. Gretter captured the essence of a summer day on the river in this photograph, taken around 1910. Photograph courtesy of Kentucky Historical Society.

Frankfort

A PICTORIAL HISTORY

**STUART SPRAGUE/
ELIZABETH PERKINS**

DESIGN BY JAMIE BACKUS

DONNING COMPANY/PUBLISHERS
VIRGINIA BEACH, VIRGINIA

When a train rumbles down the main street of Frankfort, it dominates the cityscape, not to mention that it ties up traffic. But few trains turned heads the way that The General did on July 30, 1962, during the Centennial of the Civil War. Governor Bert Combs waves a greeting while, *to his left,* his press secretary Ed Easterly looks on. Other onlookers are unidentified. Photograph by Charles B. Stone; courtesy of George H. Yater.

 For information, write: The Donning Company/Publishers, Inc., 5041 Admiral Wright Road, Virginia Beach, Virginia 23462.

Library of Congress Cataloging in Publication Data:

Sprague, Stuart, 1937-
Frankfort, a pictorial history.

Includes index.
1. Frankfort, Ky.—History—Pictorial works. I. Perkins, Elizabeth, joint author. II. Title. F459.F8S68 976.9'432 80-23571
ISBN 0-89865-003-8

Printed in United States of America

ONE WAY

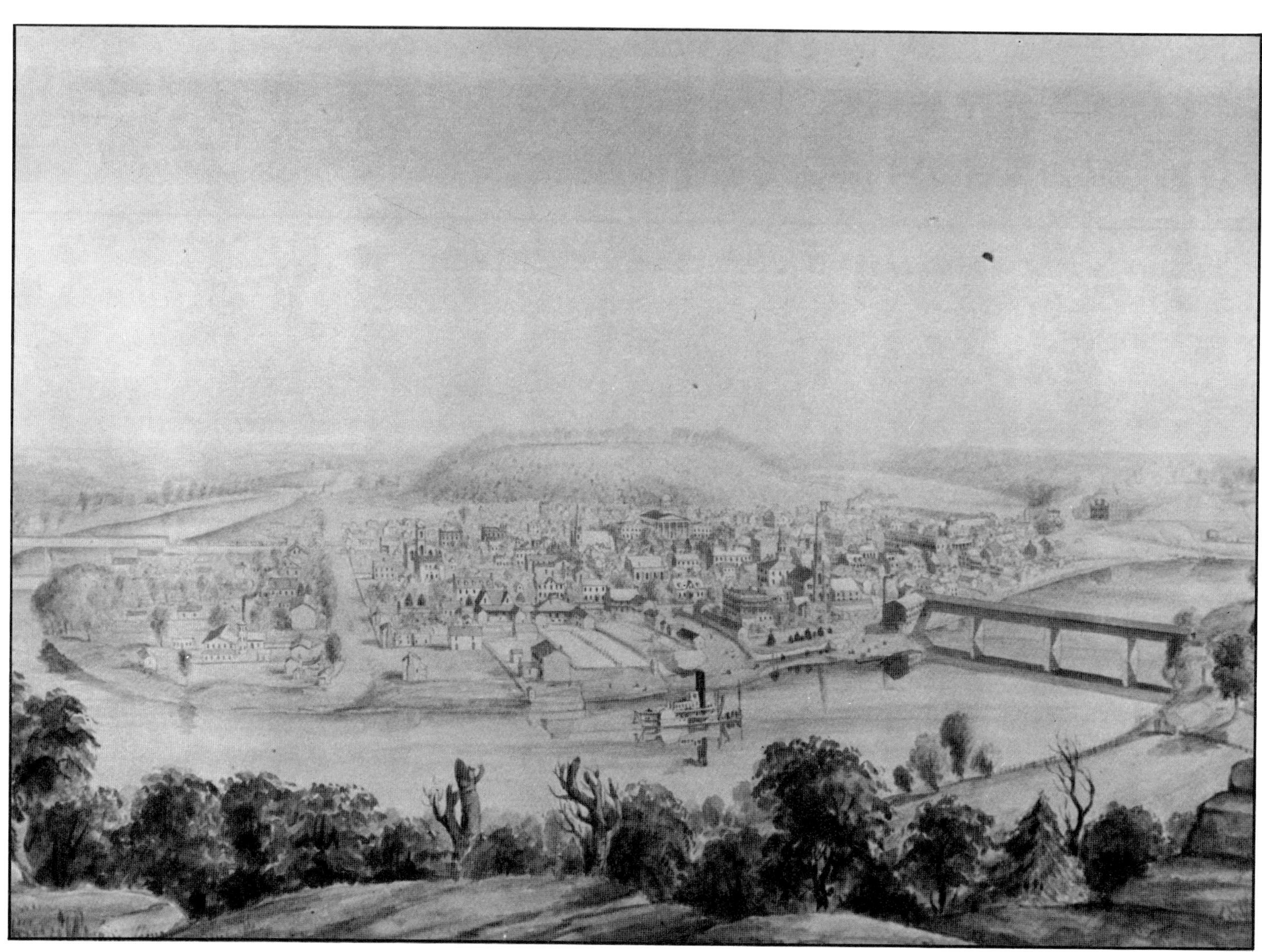

This extraordinary bird's-eye view by S.I.M. Major dates from the Civil War period and before the Confederates burned the covered railroad bridge in October 1862. The bridge, *left*, demarks Broadway. The first broad street coming towards the viewer is Wilkinson. Just to the left of Wilkinson near the water's edge smoke rises from the Cotton Factory. Behind the factory runs Wapping Street. The two large houses on Wilkinson beyond the factory are the Orlando Brown House and Liberty Hall. Starting from the bridge at the end of St. Clair Street, *right*, one can see smoke rising from the woollen factory just to the left of the entrance. Following along St. Clair Street one spots the spire and edifice of the Catholic Church and beyond it the Court House. Continuing along St. Clair one runs across the Capitol. Running one's finger in the direction of the railroad bridge to the left, one sees two spires, the first of the Episcopal Church and the other of the Presbyterian Church. The street to the right of the steamboat in the foreground is Washington Street, and the residence between that spot and the Court House is the Terraces, built in 1848 for Philip Swigert of the Farmers Bank. The State Arsenal (1850) is visible directly above the nearest pier of the St. Clair Street Bridge. The large building approximately midway between the Arsenal and the Court House on St. Clair Street is the Capitol Hotel. The Craw is the area of small residences and undeveloped land on the far side of the Capitol, to the hill behind it and to the river on the left. Photograph courtesy of Mrs. Perry Rogers.

Contents

Foreword

I first saw Frankfort in 1928 when I clambered down the long hill aboard the interurban car which ran between the Capital City and Lexington. Planted on the banks of the Kentucky River on an island of land which spreads out between the eastern and western limestone bluffs, for over two centuries the city has generated a history of economics, politics, human successes and failures, of crises, and deep tragedy.

It is doubtful whether the founders of Frankfort as the capital of Kentucky paused to consider that the river would be both a unifying and terrifying force in the city's future. From the distant eastern spine of the Cumberland Plateau to the lowlands of the Ohio it thrusts its way like a great geological lacing cord through the Commonwealth's heartland. Its waters tumble off steep mountainsides past humble hill country homes, off bluegrass tablelands with the rich pastures, sprawling fields and Greek revival mansions, but always off the continuing pageantry of Kentucky human triumph and comedy. In-and-out of season the Kentucky has poured its flood waters over Frankfort streets and through residential doorways to remind citizens and officials alike of the tremendous forces locked in the upstream countryside.

Gazing down from the western overlook on the Frankfort panorama the historian cannot refrain from reminiscing about the city's past. Across the way on the opposite bluff lie the remains of Daniel and Rebecca Boone amidst an assembly of Frankfort's departed men and women who once gave the town a rich human quality. Off to the side rises the stately dome of the elegant Old Capitol which memorializes not only the earlier acts of government with moments of success and failure, but also the tragedies of human shortsightedness and penuriousness, and of violence. Off to the side stood the house in which Solomon P Sharp was murdered, an act immortalized in history and literature. Out front a bronze plaque marks the spot where William Goebel was felled by an unidentified assassin. This tragedy marked a watershed in Kentucky history between an old-fashioned and sometimes rapacious past, and a chaotic future. In more chaste fashion the dome sits atop Gideon Shryock's classic structure which thrust the Commonwealth into a new period of Greek revival granduer and out of an era of Georgian architectural bastardy.

Rising out of the plain, like a Grecian temple in Attica, the modern Office Plaza sits on or near the old Craw. It has sharply reversed the course of history for this infamous spot. Here it was that log men at the end of perilous journeys down from the mountains aboard bucking log rafts caroused nights through in the brothels. John Fox, Jr., gave a brief glimpse of this human pageantry in his *Little Shepherd of Kingdom Come.*

Throughout its existence Frankfort has been a mixing town where proud aristocrats bearing the names of Brown, Scott, Taylor, and Wesiger mingled only distantly with men named Baker, Richardson, Turner, Lynch, Wright, Salyers, and Combs. It has been a place where country legislators strolled along the streets every two years, and sat in statehouse chambers raising points of order in furious oratorical debates over "pints of law."

It seems almost sacreligious that everyday commercial life flowed on in an environment of politics, governmental functions, and the perpetual self-seeking in the offices of constitutional officials. There were distillers, shoemakers, fishing tackle manufacturers, bankers, and servicemen, all of whom lined the streets with buildings and commercial signs. These gave the town economic and social continuity which leveled out the bi-ennial frenzy of the comings and goings of legislators, lobbyists, and citizens seeking passage or defeat of laws. With it all Frankfort streets flowed with the mundane affairs of people at home making livings like other Kentuckians in less politically charged environments.

Frankfort has been a city undergoing constant change. It has evolved through many chrysallis stages with government outgrowing buildings and constructing others to house expanding departments and to accommodate new ones. These changes have created a physical record which could be caught successfully through the camera lense. The graphic portrayal of Kentucky's Capital City is a vital part of the history of the Cmmonwealth.

No longer do the interurban cars rumble down the hill to the streets of Frankfort; instead the roads are crowded with state employee cars and trucks arriving and fleeing the city. The town itself has scaled the bluffs to be surrounded by subdivisions and shopping malls, even state office buildings have popped up above the surrounding hills. The throb of Kentucky's political life emanates from Frankfort, and no longer is there talk of moving the Capitol to a larger city. In this age of kaleidescopic change and expansion, only can a full visual concept of the past be recorded in photographs, and these become as precious visual documents as the manuscript records reposing in the Historical Society and the State Archives.

Thomas D. Clark

KENTUCK

Introduction

Free street fairs were held on the Capitol grounds beginning in 1899 and running through about 1904. The program for the 1900 fair lists balloon ascensions, trapeze artists, fireworks, and a "few novel and elegant entertainments, which are select," such as Bascoe the Snake Eater, The Cosmo-Palace Terpsichorean, and The Gypsy Camp, plus promises that "all fakirs have been rigidly excluded." One long-time resident remembers Nick Carter jumping into a barrel of water four-feet deep from a height of 112 feet as the Italian band struck up "Under the Double Eagle." Photograph courtesy of Kentucky Historical Society.

Frankfort from the time of General James Wilkinson onward has been a plucky town. In the early 1790s, when Danville and Lexington were vying to be selected as capital of the new state, the upstart city of Frankfort seized the prize. In a show of amazing public spirit and civic pride, as Kerr's *History* labels it, the town of approximately two hundred offered ten boxes of glass, fifteen hundred pounds of nails, the use of a saw mill, two horses and a cart, a donation of land, and 166 2/3 dollars worth of locks and hinges, stone, and lumber. Frankfort was the highest bidder.

Whenever the state capitol building burned or some other convenient excuse arose, larger towns attempted to take the seat of government away, but Frankfort has endured as governmental center.

All state capitals are specialized cities with rhythmic patterns of activity occasioned by the meetings of the legislature. In recent years the rhythm has been muted due to the large number of year-round governmental workers. It is a physical impossibility to break the speed limit when leaving Frankfort on a weekday between 3:00 and 5:30 P.M.. Gone is the day when the *State Journal* might report, as it did in 1910, that "the L & N Station yesterday looked as if the whole town were moving out, such a crowd of legislators and their wives and their baggage left on the morning trains."

That seasonal hegira increased the importance of the local inns and taverns. A visitor in the mid-1790s reported that the town "was very crowded at this time, on account of the Legislature sitting." He added that he had "put up at Mr. Weisiger's Tavern, the best of the town, and very good one it is," for here "the Governor and most of the members of the Legislature put up." Soon a Governor's Mansion would be provided.

The public inn was all-important; here were held public entertainments, auctions, stockholders' meetings, and public dinners. Later on, dentists and photographers would rent rooms for the legislative session. Frankfort's four public inns of 1809 impressed one tourist as being "in point of size, accommodation, and attendance" unsurpassed in America.

In the mid-1820s one E. Stanley wrote that Frankfort is "only kept alive by the sessions of the Legislature and courts of Law." Though Stanley is guilty of exaggeration, there is no question that much of Frankfort's flavor is derived from its governmental connection, best symbolized by the appearance of the state Capitol on the city seal. From the 1790s to 1937 the State Penitentiary was located at Frankfort, and over time numerous other state institutions, including Kentucky State University, have become part of Frankfort.

There is, and always has been, however, another side to Frankfort. Statistics indicate that in the mid-1960s some 1,500 employees worked in Frankfort area distilleries, and that as early as 1820 some twenty thousand bushels of corn and rye were consumed annually by Frankfort's five distilleries. From the first there was a commercial side to the capital city; its location on the Kentucky River made the fledgling city more accessible to Pittsburgh and the Northeast than Lexington was. Indeed, French General Collot was of the opinion in 1796 that "it is probable that in ten years this town will have thrice the population and wealth of Lexington."

Though Collot's prophecy was not fulfilled, it was not for lack of pluck. The 1786 law creating Frankfort had called for a ferry across the Kentucky; by 1809 a bridge of boats traversed the river, and that in turn was followed by a bridge.

Businessmen encouraged the improvement of transportation and commercial facilities. Daniel Weisiger, who owned Weisiger's Inn, was the first to sign a 1799 subscription list to build a public market; he was also at one time a director of the volunteer fire department. Leaders of the Frankfort community had a stake in community improvement.

A steady progression of steamboats began to arrive at the landing in the 1820s, and the 1830s saw the coming of the railroad, the beginning of work on Dam and Lock #4, and a series of turnpikes the hub of which was Frankfort. The 628 inhabitants of 1800 became 1,917 in 1840. Such numbers exaggerate the disruption caused by the increase, for Frankfort had been fortunate almost up to the present moment to have had available always an area of free land. The increase was housed through area expansion rather than by tearing down existing housing.

Craw in the 1820s was best known for its pond, where duck hunting was good; Bellepoint was a "wild woods." Frankfort had only three "positive streets": Main, St. Clair, and Wapping. A city resident of 1830 was optimistic about the city's future, declaring that "the prospects of Frankfort were never better....Business has taken an astonishing impulse, several houses are building, the streets are undergoing repairs—in a word the sound of the axe and the hammer are everywhere to be heard." The word "axe," the mass of forest in the 1841 view of Frankfort, and the blank spaces on the 1854 Hart and Mapother map all indicate an abundance of building sites available. The building of the new Capitol on the south side of the river early in the twentieth century encouraged real estate development there. Frankfort continued to grow until 1910, after which time it entered a period of low growth (averaging less than 315 people per decade for the next forty years). Annexation is responsible for the apparent, but not actual, population jump from 11,916 to 18,365 between 1950 and 1960. The 1970 figure was 21,356, and the 1976 estimate of 23,150 (released in January 1979) leads one to expect Frankfort's 1980 population to be between 24,000 and 25,000.

The photographs that follow celebrate nearly two hundred years of Frankfort: its landmarks, people, shops, catastrophes, and triumphs. Fortunately, the photographic record of Frankfort is fairly complete. The Commonwealth of Kentucky had the foresight to purchase the negatives of E. C. Wolff, H. A. Gretter, and the Cusick Studio. Frankfort's beauty and history made the city popular with postcard companies and visiting photographers, many of whom recorded their impressions on glass plate or nitrate negatives. In a special category belongs Paul Sawyier, whose impressionistic artwork so well captures the fragrance of turn-of-the-century Frankfort. Residents and visitors will recognize many of the structures, for many still stand, though with different names on the doors. But by casting one's eyes above street level, one discovers, frequently, the original name of the building and the date of construction. Frankfort's many historic buildings give the past a presence that is unusual for capital cities.

Frankfort has fared well in terms of the written record as well, with the works of Willard Rouse Jillson and L. Frank Johnson (recently reprinted) and the more specialized works of Henry-Russell Hitchcock on state capitols and Arthur F. Jones on Paul Sawyier. Of special note are the oral interviews carried out in 1886 in conjunction with the Centennial celebration, so that "something more enduring—something that would not perish with the hour" would be preserved. These have proved most valuable.

We have purposely kept this volume from being a series of pictures of the "great men" who are so prominent in the history of the capital city and in many cases sleep in the Frankfort Cemetery. Rather this portrait of Frankfort attempts to capture the spirit of the city as the men and women of their day might have viewed it. We have gained a greater appreciation of the city—its triumphs and tribulations and its photographers—through working on this volume.

To the people of Frankfort we dedicate this book.

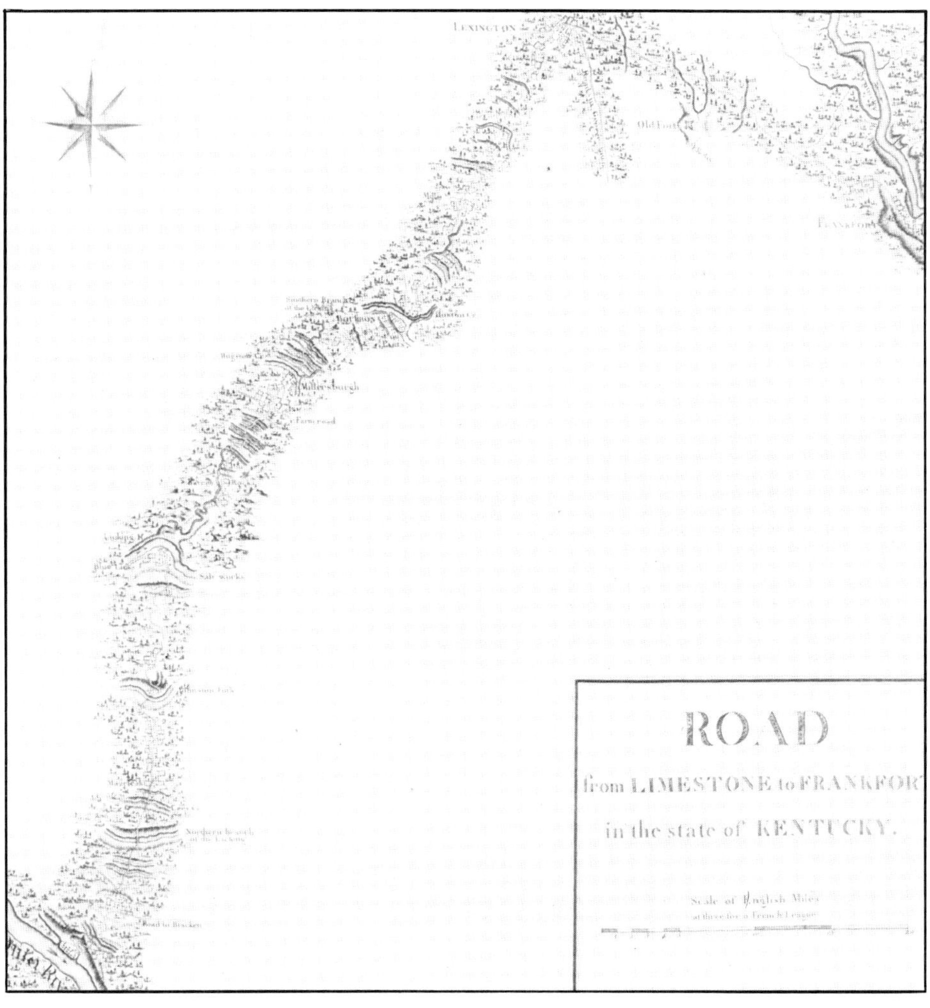

This detailed 1796 map indicates the route of travel between Maysville (Limestone) and Frankfort, and was the work of General Collot, who was spying out the country for the French. The fact that Frankfort could be reached by water as well as by an abominable road made it attractive to men with a commercial interest. Map from *A Journey in North America*, 1826, rpt. 1924; courtesy of University of Kentucky, Rare Book Room.

Between 1792, when Frankfort became the capital city, and the time an appropriate building was constructed, the Love House served as a temporary state house. Elizabeth Love and Margaretta Mason Brown organized what was perhaps the earliest Sunday School west of the mountain. The Love House, built in 1784 as a residence for General James Wilkinson, was razed in 1870. Illustration courtesy of Kentucky Historical Society.

FIRST (PERMANENT) STATE-HOUSE, FRANKFORT, KY.

The first known illustration of a Frankfort building appeared in 1796, in *New York Magazine, or Literary Repository*. Illustrator/historian Benson J. Lossing derived this version from that earlier view. This first permanent State House burned in late 1813 despite the availability of a Philadelphia-bought fire engine that had been purchased two years previously. Illustration from Lossing, *Encyclopedia of American History*.

Pictorial History

An act for establishing a town on the lands of James Wilkinson, in Fayette county, and a ferry across Kentucky river.

Town of Frankfort, in Fayette county, Kentucky, established.

I. *Be it enacted by the General Assembly,* That one hundred acres of land in the county of Fayette, the property of James Wilkinson, which have been laid off into lots and streets, shall be vested in Caleb Wallace, Thomas Marshall, Joseph Crocket, John Fowler, junior, John Craig, Robert Johnston, and Benjamin Roberts, (of Jefferson) gentlemen, trustees, and shall be established a town by the name of Frankfort. The said trustees, or a majority of them, shall within six months after passing of this act, sell at public auction, all the lots within the said town, which have not been heretofore disposed of by the said James Wilkinson, advertising the time and place of such sale at the door of the courthouse of the said county of Fayette, on two successive court days. The purchaser shall hold the said lots respectively, subject to the condition of building on each a dwelling house, sixteen feet square, with a brick or stone chimney, to be finished fit for habitation within two years from the day of sale; and the said trustees, or a major part of them, shall convey the said lots to the purchasers in fee, subject to the condition aforesaid, and pay the money arising therefrom to the said James Wilkinson, or his legal representatives; the said trustees, or a major part of them, shall have power to settle all disputes concerning the bounds of the said lots, and to establish such regulations for the regular building of houses thereon, as to them shall seem best. In case of the death, removal out of the county, or other legal disability, of any one or more of the said trustees, it shall be lawful for the remaining trustees to supply such vacancy; and the persons so chosen, shall have the same power as the trustees appointed by this act. The purchasers of the said lots, so soon as they shall have built upon and saved the same according to the conditions of their respective deeds of conveyance, shall enjoy all the privileges which the inhabitants of other towns in this state, not incorporated, hold and enjoy. If the purchaser of any lot shall fail to build thereon within the time before limited, the said trustees, or a major part of them, may thereupon enter into such lot, and sell the same again, and apply the money for the benefit of the inhabitants of the said town.

Ferry established across Kentucky river at Frankfort.

II. *And be it further enacted,* That a public ferry shall be constantly kept across the Kentucky river, from the lands of the said James Wilkinson, in the town of Frankfort, to the opposite shore, and the rates for passing the same be as followeth: For a man, four pence, and for a horse the same; and for the transportation of tobacco, wheel carriages, cattle and other beasts, the ferry keeper may demand and take the same rates as are allowed by law at other ferries. If the ferry keeper shall demand or receive from any person or persons whatsoever, any greater rates than are hereby allowed, he shall for every offence, forfeit and pay to the party grieved, the ferriage demanded or received, and ten shillings; to be recovered with costs before a justice of the peace of the county where the offence shall be committed.

Frankfort donated the Public Square for governmental use. This land was used not only for the State House, but also for other state buildings, including the first Kentucky Penitentiary, 1799. Illustration from Sneed, *History of the Penitentiary,* 1860; courtesy of University of Kentucky, Special Collections.

When the Virginia legislature passed this 1786 act, no one imagined that in six years the town would become the state capital of Kentucky. General James Wilkinson not only gave the town Wilkinson Street, but also Ann Street, named after his wife. From Hening, *The Statutes at Large.*

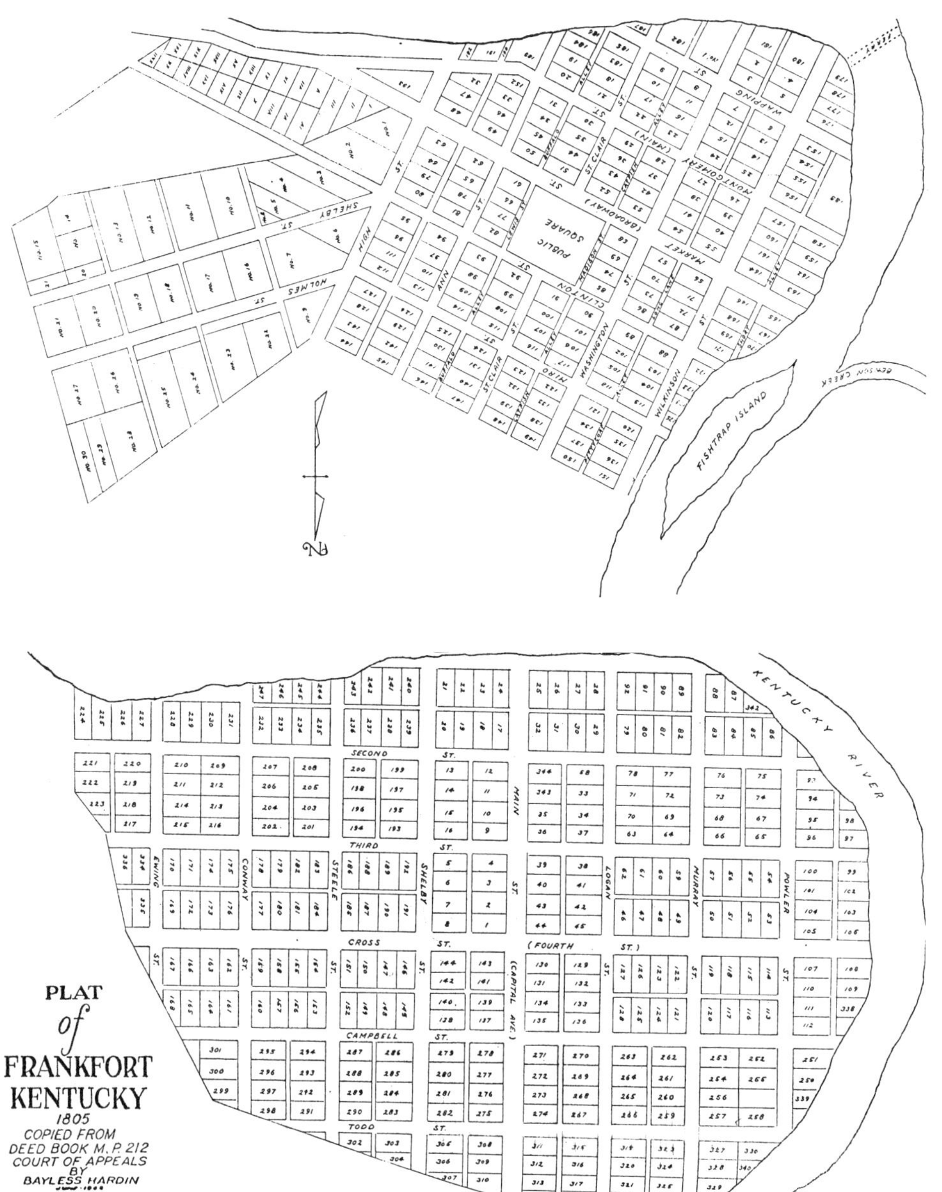

Bayless Hardin's rendition of the 1805 Frankfort Plat clearly shows the location of the Public Square and each of the numbered lots. Note that Broadway was then called Market, and Main Street was then called Montgomery. Map from *Register of the Kentucky Historical Society*.

Hardin's rendition of South Frankfort shows Fourth Street as Cross Street and Capitol Avenue as Main Street. An 1854 map indicates that half a century later there were still few houses built in this area. Map from *Register of the Kentucky Historical Society*.

Augured cedar pipes transported water to Frankfort from 1804 to 1886. The water source was Cedar Cove, three miles away. Frankfort thus had with the Frankfort Water Company the first waterworks in the state. Photograph courtesy of Kentucky Historical Society.

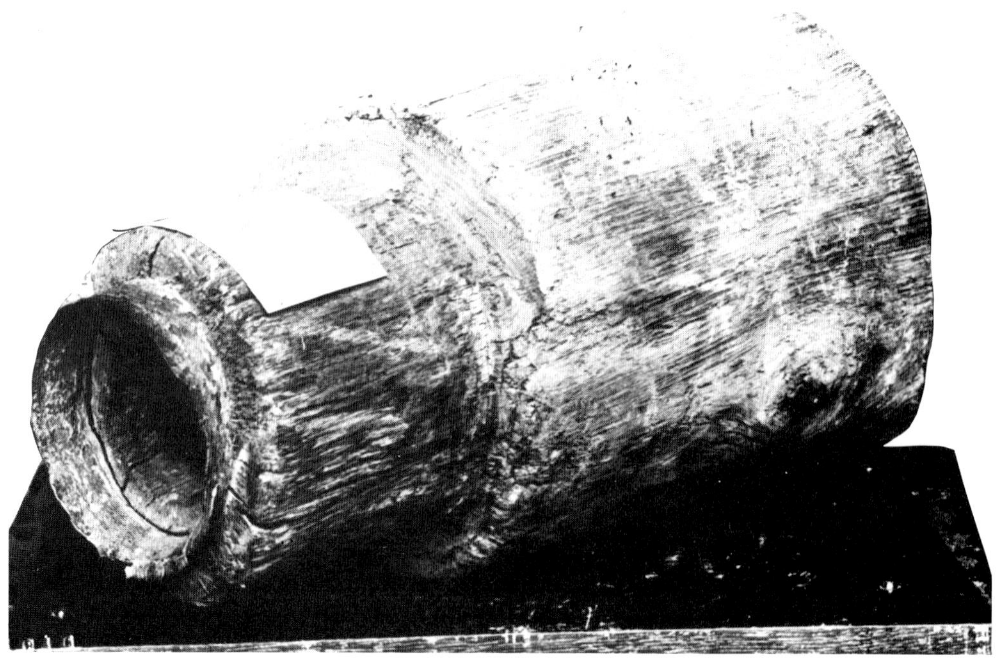

The old Governor's Mansion, styled the Governor's Palace on the 1854 map, was used as the official residence of Kentucky's chief executive between 1798 and 1914. The fence and elaborate front porch on this postcard postmarked 1912 have long since disappeared, as has the cornice at the eaves line. From the Sprague Postcard Collection.

This view was taken shortly before the Governor's Mansion became the residence of the lieutenant governor. The windows are shuttered, and the trees show the effects of forty years of additional growth. Photograph courtesy of J. Winston Coleman Kentuckiana Collection, Frances Carrick Thomas Library, Transylvania University.

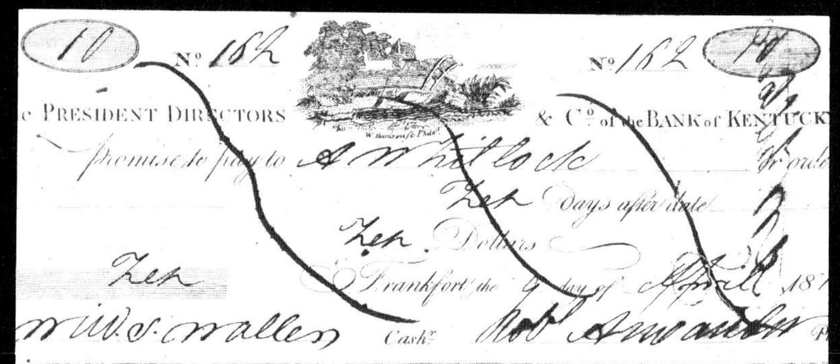

As capital city, Frankfort became a financial center. Banks of the War of 1812 period printed both checks and bank notes, such as these printed for the Frankfort and Bank of Kentucky banks. Bank notes courtesy of Alfred G. Hortmann, St. Louis.

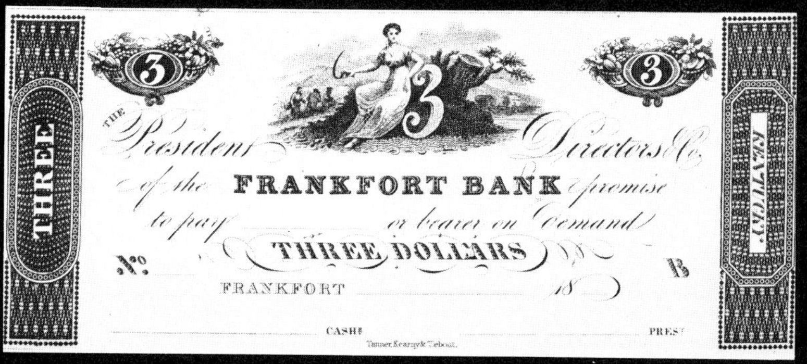

The need for a new Capitol became even more pressing when the meeting house, in which the House of Representatives met temporarily, burned. The meeting house was a church building used by various denominations, and was constructed in 1812 on the southwest corner of the Public Square, from the proceeds of a lottery. The governor appointed the building's trustees. The Frankfort *Argus* expressed the mood of the inhabitants when it reported that "property owners have remained in painful suspense"; but upon word that a new building was forthcoming, "they now feel relieved." Subscription courtesy of University of Kentucky Special Collections; Illustration from Collins *History of Kentucky*.

SUBSCRIPTION

FOR REBUILDING THE CAPITOL

IN THE TOWN OF FRANKFORT.

WHEREAS, by an act passed at the last session of the General Assembly, the sum of three thousand dollars is appropriated to the Trustees of Frankfort, for the purpose of commencing the rebuilding the Capitol; and the Trustees feeling a deep interest, in common with the citizens of Franklin and the adjoining counties, in having the Capitol rebuilt as soon as practicable, have, in pursuance of the wishes of the citizens of this place, as expressed at a public meeting, ordered subscription papers to be printed and circulated to afford all persons an opportunity of subscribing who may feel interested in effecting so desirable an object: Therefore,

We, the subscribers, do hereby bind ourselves, our heirs, executors and administrators, to pay to the Trustees of the Town of Frankfort, or their successors, the several sums of money annexed to our respective names, at the several periods hereinafter mentioned, viz: *One third* of the sum subscribed, to be paid on the first day of March next; *one third* on the first day of July, and the remaining *third* on the first day of November.

FRANKFORT, JANUARY 3d, 1826.

The Kentucky Penitentiary's towers would be a landmark until the flood waters of 1937 encouraged the legislature to replace the prison. A move to preserve the entrance met with temporary success, but the towers were later demolished. Illustration from Sneed, *History of the Penitentiary*, 1860; courtesy of University of Kentucky, Special Collections.

This enlarged inset from Munsell's updated Kentucky map (the 1834 update of the well known 1818 map) shows a number of features that would later disappear. Fishtrap Island, which reportedly was used both by pioneers and Indians, would succumb with the completion of Dam #4 in 1844. The 1806 Court House, "a plain brick building" with "a piazza of five arches" that opened into the court room was located on the corner of Lewis and Broadway. Already Gideon Shyrock's architectural rendering for a new Court House had been approved. The market would be removed from the middle of Broadway when the railroad came to town in 1835. Map courtesy of University of Kentucky, Special Collections.

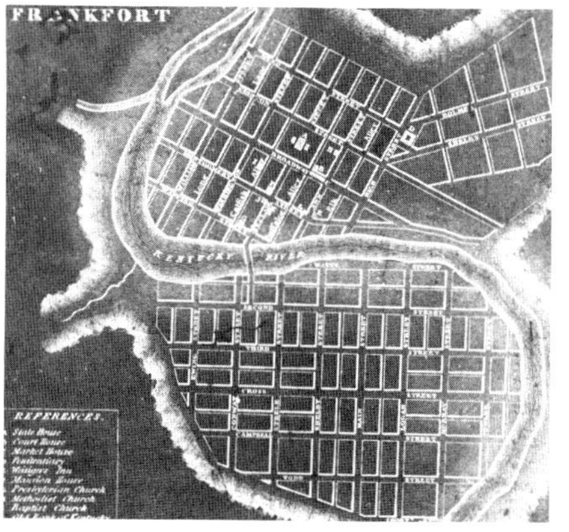

These sketches preserve a sense of what the first trains looked like. The Logan and the Boone were but the first of a long line of locomotives that linked Frankfort to surrounding towns and cities. Illustrations from *Register of the Kentucky Historical Society*.

LEXINGTON AND OHIO RAIL ROAD WAREHOUSE,

FRANKFORT, January 14 1836

RECEIVED *from* **P. DUDLEY & Co.** *in good order, the following described packages, marked as per margin, viz:*

J W H & Son	1 Hhd Sugar 1150
	[illegible]

Which I promise to deliver in like good order, and without delay, (unavoidable accidents excepted,) to [illegible] *on Rail Road at* Lexington *he paying* [illegible] *cents per 100 lbs. for carriage of the same.*

(SIGNED DUPLICATES.)

[illegible signature]

Hodges, Todd & Pruett, Printers, Frankfort, Ky.

LEXINGTON AND OHIO RAILROAD.

M'KEE & SWIGERT'S WAY-BILL FOR PASSENGERS.

Railroad Office, Lexington **Ky.** April 14 **1845.**

Passengers' Names.	Where From.	Where To.	No. Seats.	Dolls.	Cts.	Remarks.
WAY FARE,				1	25	
Higgins			2	2	50	
Mathews			1	1	25	
[illegible]			1	1	25	
Colored Boy			1	1	25	
Berry			1	1	25	
Allen			1	1	25	
				10	00	

Freight was important to the Louisville & Ohio Railroad. Service was swift, though not always reliable. In March 1836 the young company had its first accident just a few miles from Frankfort. Receipts courtesy of Kentucky Historical Society.

With improved rail, river, and turnpike connections, Frankfort became more accessible. The *Medium* was but one of a number of steamers that plyed the river between Frankfort and the Ohio. Shipping order courtesy of Kentucky Historical Society.

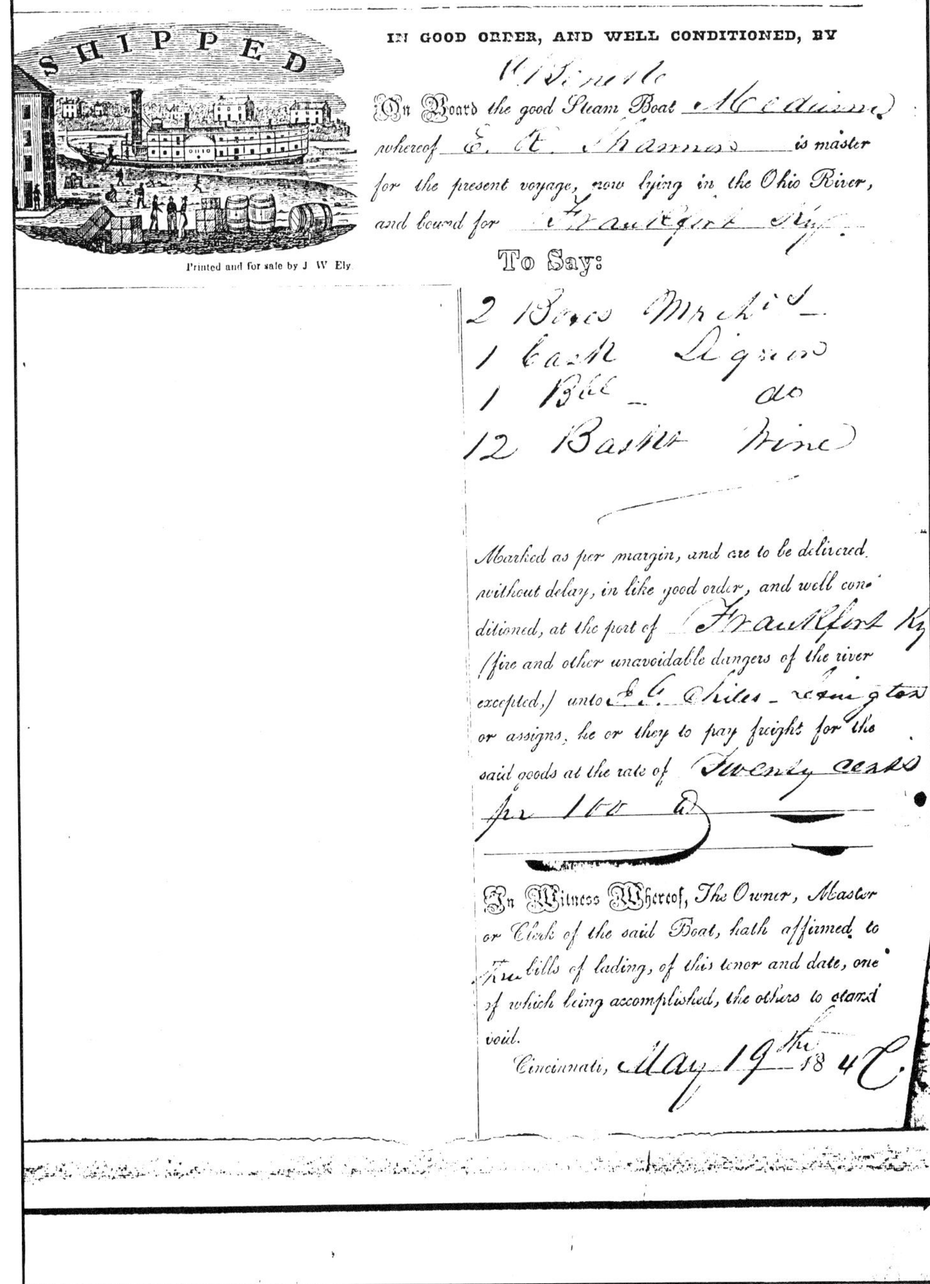

SHIPPED

Printed and for sale by J. W. Ely.

IN GOOD ORDER, AND WELL CONDITIONED, BY

[illegible]

On Board the good Steam Boat Medium *whereof* E. R. [illegible] *is master for the present voyage, now lying in the Ohio River, and bound for* Frankfort Ky.

To Say:

2 Boxes [illegible]
1 Cask [illegible]
1 Bbl do
12 Baskets Wine

Marked as per margin, and are to be delivered without delay, in like good order, and well conditioned, at the port of Frankfort Ky *(fire and other unavoidable dangers of the river excepted,) unto* E. C. Chiles – Lexington *or assigns, he or they to pay freight for the said goods at the rate of* Twenty cents per 100 lb

In Witness Whereof, The Owner, Master or Clerk of the said Boat, hath affirmed to two *bills of lading, of this tenor and date, one of which being accomplished, the others to stand void.*

Cincinnati, May 19th 1846

These beautiful banknotes emphasize the agricultural roots of Kentucky wealth. The originals are two-toned to make counterfeiting more difficult. The portraits are likenesses of Governor John J. Crittenden and his wife. Crittenden resigned his post in 1850 to become attorney general under President Fillmore, a position he had earlier held under Tippecanoe and Tyler too. He would later be remembered for the Crittenden Compromise, which sought to head off the Civil War. Though in ill health, Crittenden appeared in public during the war, boosting the morale of Union soldiers stationed in Kentucky. He died in the summer of 1863. The notes, printed by the still-extant American Bank Note Company, came in sheets of four which were cut into individual notes. Sheet courtesy of University of Kentucky; single notes collection of Alfred G. Hortmann, St. Louis.

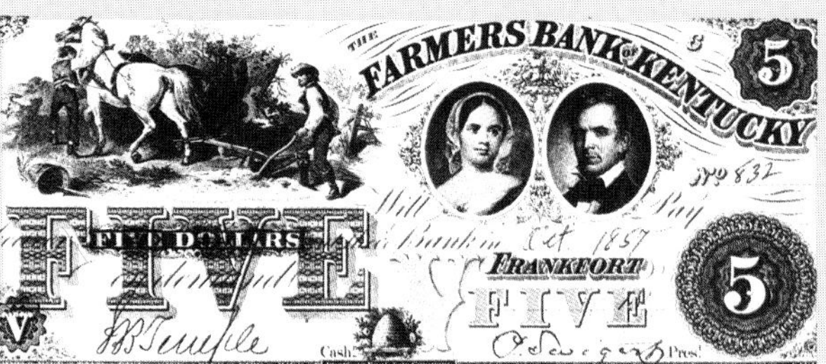

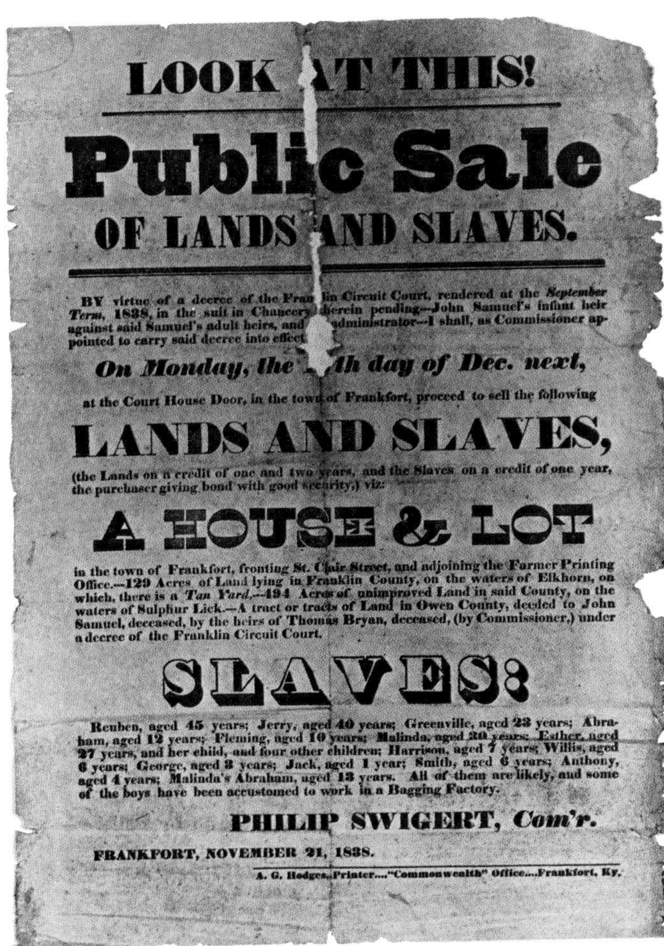

LOOK AT THIS!

Public Sale

OF LANDS AND SLAVES.

BY virtue of a decree of the Fran lin Circuit Court, rendered at the *September Term,* 1838, in the suit in Chancery therein pending--John Samuel's infant heir against said Samuel's adult heirs, and administrator--I shall, as Commissioner appointed to carry said decree into effect,

On Monday, the [illegible]th day of Dec. next,

at the Court House Door, in the town of Frankfort, proceed to sell the following

LANDS AND SLAVES,

(the Lands on a credit of one and two years, and the Slaves on a credit of one year, the purchaser giving bond with good security,) viz:

A HOUSE & LOT

in the town of Frankfort, fronting St. Clair Street, and adjoining the Farmer Printing Office.--129 Acres of Land lying in Franklin County, on the waters of Elkhorn, on which, there is a *Tan Yard,*--494 Acres of unimproved Land in said County, on the waters of Sulphur Lick.--A tract or tracts of Land in Owen County, deeded to John Samuel, deceased, by the heirs of Thomas Bryan, deceased, (by Commissioner,) under a decree of the Franklin Circuit Court.

SLAVES:

Reuben, aged 45 years; Jerry, aged 40 years; Greenville, aged 23 years; Abraham, aged 12 years; Fleming, aged 10 years; Malinda, aged 30 years; Esther, aged 27 years, and her child, and four other children; Harrison, aged 7 years; Willis, aged 6 years; George, aged 3 years; Jack, aged 1 year; Smith, aged 6 years; Anthony, aged 4 years; Malinda's Abraham, aged 13 years. All of them are likely, and some of the boys have been accustomed to work in a Bagging Factory.

PHILIP SWIGERT, *Com'r.*

FRANKFORT, NOVEMBER 21, 1838.

A. G. Hodges, Printer...."Commonwealth" Office....Frankfort, Ky.

The sale of slaves was not uncommon, as this broadside attests. Newspaper editors increased their income through job printing. Publishers came to Frankfort with the hope of becoming the state printer, and subsidies to editors who followed the party line were commonplace. A. G. Hodges of the *Commonwealth* remained public printer for a quarter century. Among the best known early newspapermen were Amos Kendall, better known for being a member of Andrew Jackson's kitchen cabinet, and Humphrey Marshall whose partisan *History of Kentucky* 1812, the first extensive history of Kentucky, is still read.

The present old Capitol dominates this 1841 engraving published in the *Ladies Repository*. On the right is the Penitentiary. Tracks run down Broadway. At the Old Market, which originally occupied Broadway between Ann and Lewis Streets, the city rented stalls to merchants and farmers. As a result of the coming of the railroad, the market was removed to the southeast corner of Broadway and Ann. By 1884 groceries replaced an open market, and the building was sold; the new owners rented space for stores. Eventually the property was purchased by the railroad and the relic demolished. Print of engraving courtesy of Kentucky Historical Society.

These two sections of Hart and Mapother's 1854 map show individual buildings. Weisiger's Inn has been replaced by the Capitol Hotel, and a railroad depot sits next to the Market House. Montgomery and Market Streets have assumed new names, and at their intersection rises the new State Arsenal. Craw, the section north and northwest of the old Capitol, is developing, whereas South Frankfort remains sparsely populated. Frankfort has been blessed with areas of underused space throughout its history, a factor which has permitted area expansion as an alternative to demolition. Map courtesy of University of Kentucky, Special Collections.

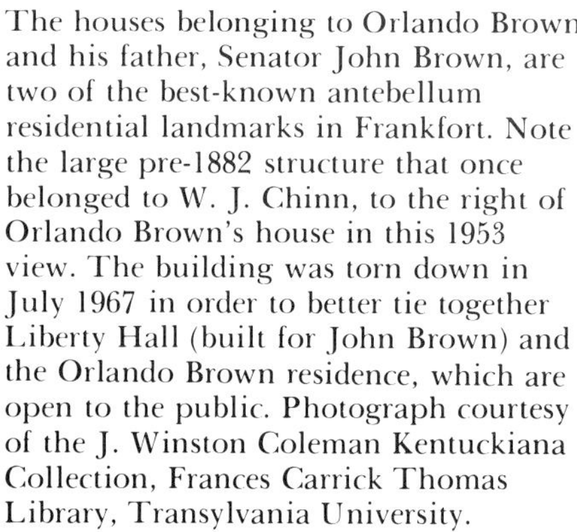

The houses belonging to Orlando Brown and his father, Senator John Brown, are two of the best-known antebellum residential landmarks in Frankfort. Note the large pre-1882 structure that once belonged to W. J. Chinn, to the right of Orlando Brown's house in this 1953 view. The building was torn down in July 1967 in order to better tie together Liberty Hall (built for John Brown) and the Orlando Brown residence, which are open to the public. Photograph courtesy of the J. Winston Coleman Kentuckiana Collection, Frances Carrick Thomas Library, Transylvania University.

Liberty Hall, the residence of Senator John Brown, is presently open to the public. Brown was a member of the Virginia Legislature and the Old Congress in the days before statehood. He served as United States senator from 1792 until 1805 and was an ardent Jeffersonian Republican. Photograph courtesy of the J. Winston Coleman Kentuckiana Collection, Frances Carrick Thomas Library, Transylvania University.

Professor B. B. Sayre taught in Frankfort from 1836 until his death in 1879. In 1836 the Reverend William Purvance and L. B. Nash merged their schools and called their new institution the Frankfort Academy. Sayre was one of the teachers. He taught where the Episcopal Church is now located, later on at 236 St. Clair Street (1842-48), and in other localities. His students included many of the leading residents of the town. Photograph by Elrod, courtesy of Kentucky Historical Society.

The National Branch Bank building at 212 St. Clair Street, which lasted from 1850 until it was razed in 1959, had a fine location next to the Court House. Until 1914 it was heated solely by open grates. The spire of the Church of the Good Shepherd can be seen peering over the doomed building in this photograph taken in the late 1950s. Photograph courtesy of Kentucky Historical Society.

The Catholics bought the old Presbyterian Church on Wapping Street, whose edifice had two doors, one for men and the other for women, Shaker style. The Catholics tore down the old church and in 1850 built this structure, which still stands. In point of time the Methodists completed their brick church building first (in 1849), replacing an 1823 structure on Ann Street between Clinton and Broadway. However, the building was consumed by fire in 1854 and the congregation settled upon a new location, Washington Street between Wapping and Main, to construct their new building. In this photograph of the Catholic Church of the Good Shepherd, the Baptist Church (1868), which has been remodelled extensively, can be seen in the background. Tradition states that the first Baptist service in Frankfort was held in 1787, long before any denomination had a church building in Frankfort. Photograph by Lester Jones, Historic American Buildings Survey; courtesy of University of Kentucky, Department of Interior Collection.

Bishop Asbury, who wrote in 1810 that in Frankfort there "are elegant accommodations provided for those who make the laws and break them, but there is no house of God," would have been pleasantly surprised if he were to come back in 1852, for in the period 1849-52, no less than four substantial church buildings were constructed. The senior of these is the Presbyterian Church (1849) which still stands. Though not entirely completed, the church was opened for a service on the occasion of President-elect Zachary Taylor's visit on his way to Washington, D.C. Photograph by Cline; courtesy of University of Kentucky Postcard Collection.

SUNDAY SCHOOL CELEBRATION,

ASCENSION CHURCH,

FRANKFORT, KY.,

WEDNESDAY, JULY 4, 1866,

(IN THE CHAPEL AT 10 1-2 O'CLOCK, A. M.)

ORDER OF EXERCISES.

1. Prayer.
2. The following Psalm will be sung to the tune ARLINGTON:

Let all the lands, with shouts of joy,
To God their voices raise:
Sing psalms in honor of His name,
And spread His glorious praise.

And let them say, how dreadful, Lord,
In all Thy works, art thou!
To Thy great power Thy stubborn foes
Shall all be forced to bow.

Through all the earth the nations round
Shall Thee their God confess;
And with glad hymns their awful dread
Of Thy great name express.

O, come! behold the works of God,
And then with me you'll own
That He to all the sons of men
Has wondrous judgment shown.

O, all ye nations! bless our God,
And loudly speak His praise:
Who keeps our souls alive, and still
Confirms our steadfast ways.

3. Reading of DECLARATION of INDEPENDENCE by GEORGE R. VALLANDINGHAM, Esq.
4. The following Psalm will be sung to the tune LAYBAN:

To bless Thy chosen race,
In mercy, Lord, incline:
And cause the brightness of Thy face
On all Thy saints to shine:

That so Thy wondrous way
May through the world be known:
While distant lands their tribute pay,
And Thy salvation own.

Let differing nations join
To celebrate Thy fame;
Let all the world, O, Lord, combine
To praise Thy glorious name.

O, let them shout and sing,
With joy and pious mirth;
For Thou, the righteous Judge and King,
Shalt govern all the earth.

Then God upon our land
Shall constant blessings shower,
And all the world in awe shall stand
Of His resistless power.

5. Address by Col. SAM'L B. CHURCHILL.
6. Doxology to "Old Hundred:"

Praise God from whom all blessings flow;
Praise Him all creatures here below;
Praise Him above, ye angelic host;
Praise Father, Son, and Holy Ghost.

The Episcopal Church of Frankfort was not organized until about 1835, but with a thousand-dollar gift from an anonymous New York donor, the denomination was able to buy a crab orchard with a law office in it, and in 1842 build a church house. John H. Hanna in 1850 put up the twenty thousand dollars for the new building, and two years and four days later the Church of the Ascension was completed. The building is being renovated. Photograph by Stuart Sprague, May 1979. Broadside courtesy of University of Kentucky, Special Collections.

First Methodist Church (1854 and 1886). The stone front was not added until 1886. Thus the need for two dates of construction. Photograph by Stuart Sprague, May 1979.

The Civil War

This view from above the railroad tracks clearly shows the tunnel that still exists. and above it the State Arsenal. The flat-topped cupola of the large structure in the middleground is the Capitol Hotel. At the water's edge, *foreground*, is a log raft not yet broken up. Along the dirt path that leads from the landing to Main Street are large timbers that had been rafted down the Kentucky. The stone building just to the left of the intersection of the road from the landing and Main Street is the old stone house (1840) as the building is now called. It was a rooming house for lumberjacks. Barges of the style that line the Kentucky River in this view were used to transport bulky goods. As early as 1805 one such vessel brought coal from Appalachian Kentucky to the capital city. The Catholic Church, the Court House, the Presbyterian and Episcopal churches, and the Capitol pierce the cityscape. Photograph courtesy of Kentucky Historical Society.

Frankfort, on the line of the railroad between Louisville and Lexington, proved a pleasant surprise for many Union soldiers. There, remembered a member of the 34th Illinois Infantry, "generous quantities of hot coffee and lunches were furnished by the kind and hospitable people, many richly dressed, intelligent ladies being among the number." A 33rd Indiana infantryman recorded the "hearty welcome" extended by "many of the loyal citizens" when the train crawled through downtown Frankfort. It was a refreshing change from their cold receptions in other portions of the Commonwealth.

For some regiments, Frankfort was more than a way station. Units were scattered throughout the area, here soldiers commanding an elevated position, there guarding the several bridges that crossed the Kentucky River in and around Frankfort. At Frankfort the 103rd Ohio Infantry received new Enfield rifles, and the area resounded with the echoes of the reports of their fire as a hundred cartridges were given per man to test his new weapon.

The burning of the railroad bridge and the inauguration of Confederate Governor Richard Hawes, both in October 1862, were high points for the Confederacy in the capital city. Those Confederate achievements were short-lived, however, as the bridge was rebuilt (though uncovered) and the Governor skedaddled before Southern sympathizers could hold their projected inaugural ball.

Within a week the bloody Battle of Perryville ended the threat of permanent Confederate conquest. In mid-February 1863 Confederate sympathizers attempted to hold a convention at the theatre building, but Colonel S. A. Gilbert scotched the conclave. He declared that "he knew the majority of them to be traitors of the most contemptible type... that they couldn't nominate men of their stripe for office, and if they did, and succeeded... they shouldn't hold office as long as a Federal regiment" was afoot in Kentucky. Sheepishly, the convention adjourned *sine die*. L. Frank Johnson, the Franklin County historian, stated that 178 men from the county volunteered for the Confederacy, while 235 volunteered for the Union.

A *carte-de-visite* shows the view down Main Street in the 1860s. Gas for illumination was introduced in Frankfort in 1848, and the lamp posts that were put up around town can be seen clearly here. Early records indicate that street lamps were not used on moonlit nights. Photograph courtesy of Kentucky Historical Society.

Another view in the 1860s shows an elegantly attired couple strolling down the street. The gentleman in his long frock coat is escorting a lady in hoop skirts. They are perhaps walking in the streets to avoid brushing up against the riffraff. Photograph courtesy of Kentucky Historical Society.

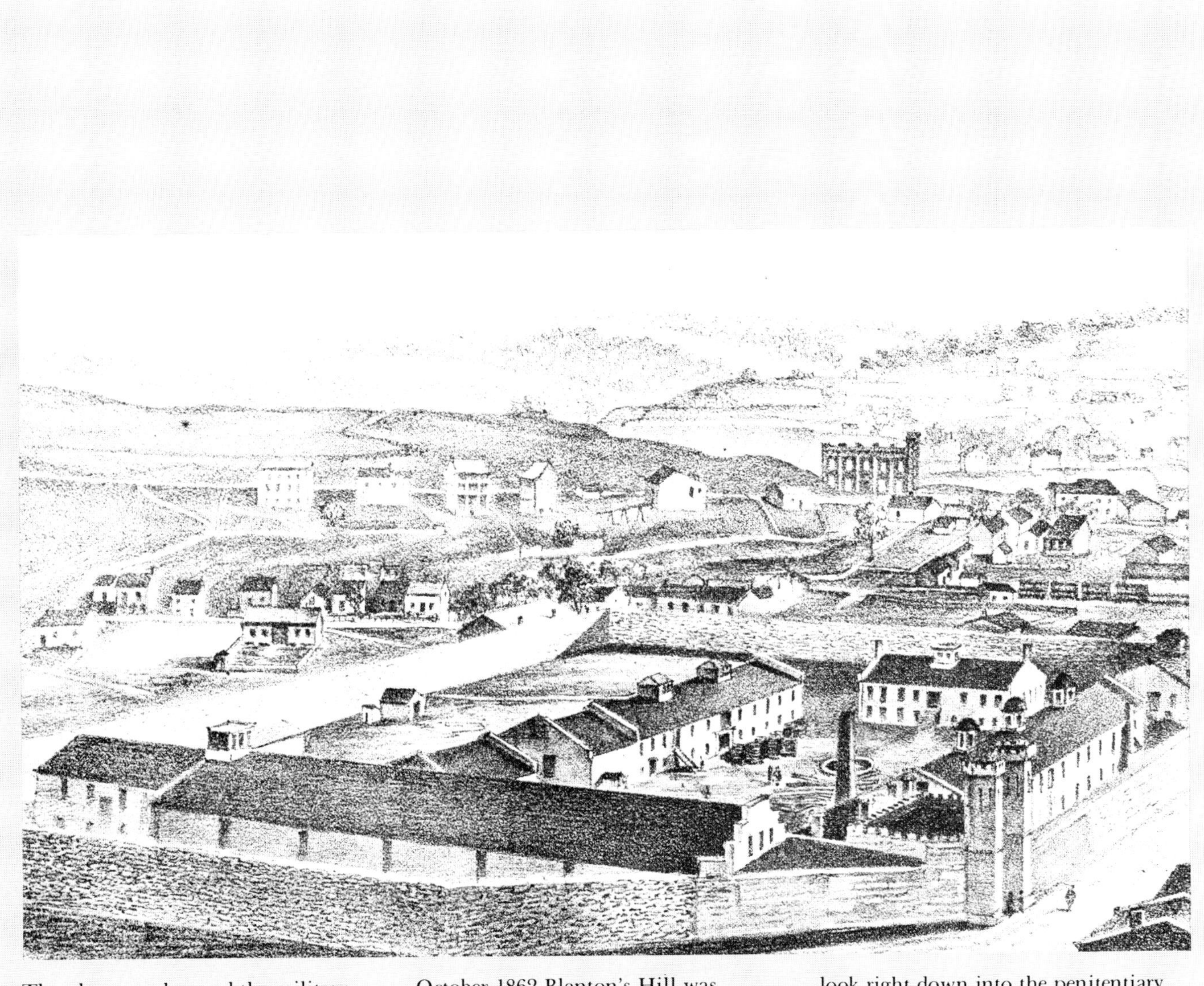

The photographer and the military officer appreciate high ground. This lithograph based on a lost 1860 photograph by C. A. Clarke was taken from the hillside behind Frankfort and in the direction of the State Arsenal that overlooks the Kentucky River. During October 1862 Blanton's Hill was occupied by Union troops. A member of the 72nd Indiana wrote that "about 8 A.M., October 8, 1862, we were marched to the top of a high hill east of town...and went into camp. Our camp ground overlooked the city...we could look right down into the penitentiary walls and see the convicts in their striped clothes at work." Lithograph from Sneed, *History of the Penitentiary*, 1860; courtesy of University of Kentucky, Special Collections.

Pennsylvania-born Daniel Boone is one of the two most famous figures connected with Kentucky's rich history. The frontiersman left for what would be Missouri in the waning years of the eighteenth century and died there in 1820. By obtaining permission from Boone's relatives and through the appropriation of funds by the Kentucky legislature, the rotting remains of Daniel and his wife Rebecca were transported to Frankfort. Business was suspended in the city on September 13, 1845, so all could attend the re-interment ceremonies at Frankfort Cemetery. In 1860 the legislature funded a monument with panels of Italian marble; the work was completed and set in place in 1862. Relic hunters defaced the monument over the years so that in 1906 the legislature appropriated two thousand dollars to replace the panels. With additional funds provided by the Rebecca Boone Chapter of the Daughters of the American Revolution, the work was forwarded and completed in 1909. Though this photograph by University of Kentucky Professor Louis E. Nollau was taken about 1909-10, the near-mint condition of the panels replicates the state of the monument in 1862. On November 2, 1862, an Ohio infantryman wrote: "Our camp is located in the suburbs of the city on the left bank of the Kentucky River. . . . On the opposite bank is a lofty bluff, almost perpendicular, at the base of which runs the Louisville and Lexington Rail Road. . . . On the Summit, amid a clump of evergreens, is the tomb of Daniel Boone. . . plainly visible from our camp." Photograph courtesy of University of Kentucky, Louis E. Nollau Collection.

Many of Frankfort's leading citizens found their final resting place in the Frankfort Cemetery. This 1857 plat lists as trustees: Mason Brown, E. H. Taylor, Henry Wingate, J. H. Hanna, Orlando Brown, P. Swigert, and H. Evans. Illustration courtesy of Kentucky Historical Society.

Right:
The Confederate Circle in 1979 was hardly recognizable. Only the monument itself was kept up. Stones leaned every which way. A subsequent visit, June, 1980, revealed the circle in pristine condition with the Stars and Bars unfurled overhead. Photograph by Stuart Sprague, 1979.

Left:
Kentucky has had an extremely rich tradition of military service. Nearly two-thirds of all troops killed in the War of 1812 were Kentuckians. Zachary Taylor, who grew up in Kentucky, parleyed his Mexican War fame into the presidency. The Legislature of 1847-48 voted for a State Monument in memory of its military dead. The sixty-five foot, more than 150-ton monument topped by a statue of Victory cost fifteen thousand dollars and was finished in June 1849. Photograph courtesy of J. Winston Coleman Kentuckiana Collection, Frances Carrick Thomas Library, Transylvania University.

Below:
The Confederate Circle at Frankfort Cemetery. Courtesy of University of Kentucky Postcard Collection.

"The Squire," J. Winston Coleman, Kentucky's leading photographer of historic sites, views the tomb of Solomon P. Sharp at Frankfort Cemetery in this 1953 photograph.

The assassination of Solomon P. Sharp as he answered the knocking at his door climaxed a period of tenseness. The Depression or Panic of 1819 led to a division of the legislature into relief and anti-relief factions. Two rival courts of appeal existed, and a Bank of the Commonwealth whose notes were not redeemable for specie, yet made receivable for taxes and all debts, created an unstable situation. The Old Court ran John J. Crittenden for the Frankfort seat in the legislature. The New Court party responded with their strongest man, Solomon P. Sharp—a colonel of the Kentucky militia, a Congressman between 1813 and 1817, a state legislator in 1809-11 and 1817-18, attorney general of Kentucky from 1820-24. Charges of vote-buying were rife. Sharp nosed out Crittenden by sixty-nine votes. Threats on Sharp's life were common. Sharp spent the nights of November 5-6, 1825, buttonholing politicians with a view towards forwarding his candidacy for speaker. Around midnight he returned to his Madison Street home, which faced the public square. About two A.M., November 6, 1825, Sharp was called to his door and stabbed to death without warning. Four thousand dollars in reward money was offered, and soon the trail led to Jereboam O. Beauchamp, whose hatred for Sharp was bottomed on Sharp's bad treatment of Ann Cook, whom Beauchamp had married in 1824. Beauchamp confessed. The sensational trial filled the Court House. When Beauchamp was found guilty and his wife innocent, the couple took poison, but failed to cheat the hangman. Then on the day of the projected public hanging, they tried again by stabbing themselves. The two died that day, the hangman barely managing to hang Beauchamp before the assassin died of his self-inflicted wound. Photograph courtesy of J. Winston Coleman Kentuckiana Collection, Frances Carrick Thomas Library, Transylvania University.

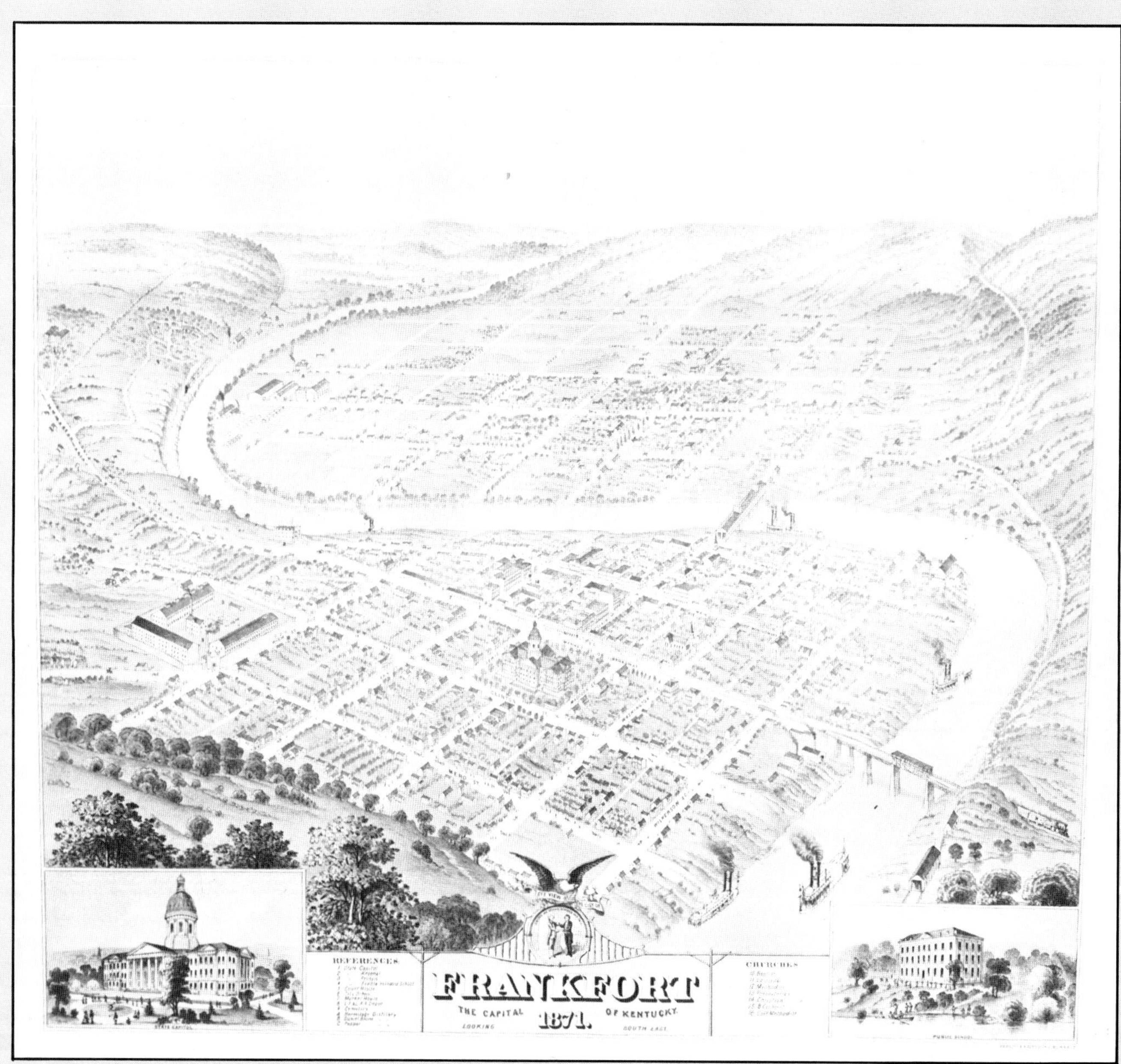

Bird's-eye views were popular in the late nineteenth century. This 1871 Frankfort bird's-eye, like most, flattens the topography. The Capitol that was never completely built is featured as an insert and in the body. The plan was to raze the old Capitol. Only the East Wing of the projected public building was constructed, and it is now the home of the Kentucky Historical Society. Bird's-eye view courtesy of Kentucky Historical Society; illustration from Collins' *History of Kentucky*.

The 1870-71 Kentucky Business Directory includes many familiar names in its Frankfort listing.

114 KENTUCKY BUSINESS DIRECTORY.

FRANKFORT.

Ackland, Wayle & Freeman, clothing, hats, caps, &c.
Adams Express Co., G. W. Owen, agent.
Allen, N., grocer.
Allen, W., boots and shoes.
Averill, W. H., drugs & musical instr's.
Ayres, Mrs. C. E., millinery.
Bachman, A., clothing, &c.
Bacon, W. R. & Co., undertakers and upholsterers.
Bank of Kentucky; A. W. Dudley, pres't, E. H. Taylor, cash.
Bates, John C., groceries and produce.
Black & Chinn, wholesale & retail coal.
Bramlett & Barrett, attorneys and counsellors at law.
Brown, John, mason.
Buckwalter, Mrs. C. E., millinery.
Burns, E., grocer.
Callery, Wm., liquors.
Capitol Hotel, A. McGill, prop'r.
Castleman, Lewis & Co., distillers.
Cavenagh, Wm., grocer.
Conery, W. B., watches, clocks, and jewelry.
Cox, L. J., paper manufacturer.
Craddock & Trabue, attorneys.
Crutcher, J. N., boots, shoes, hats, caps, school books, stationery, &c.
Crutcher, W. L., gen'l insurance ag't.
Dawson, Jas. A., gen'l insurance ag't.
Deposit Bank of Frankfort; P. Swigert, pres't, John Watson, cash.
Dudley, A. W., pres't Bank Kentucky.
Dudley, J. G. & B., planing mill.
Ellis, Mrs. M. A., millinery.
Farmers' Bank of Kentucky; T. N. Lindsay, pres't, Grant Green, cash.
Flynn, J. & W. T., coopers.
Frankf't Commonwealth, A. G. Hodges, publisher.
Gaines, Berry & Co., wholesale and retail liquors.
Gaines, W. A. & Co., distillers.
Graham, John R., undertaker and dealer in furniture.
Graham, A. J., grocer.
Gray & Walcutt, wholesale and retail grocers.
Green, Grant, cashier Farmers' Bank of Kentucky.
Greenup, W. H. & Co., dry goods, &c.
Gwin, Geo. W., hardware.
Hall, W. H., drugs.
Haley, John, boots, shoes, hats, caps, books, and stationery.
Haley, D. L., grocer.
Hardin, W. H. H., photographer.
Helms, Jno. M., boots, shoes, hats, caps, stationery, &c.
Hodges, A. G., publisher Frankfort Commonwealth.
Hodges, James A. & Co., grocers.
Holloran, John M., general store.
Holman, J. M., grocer.
Hord, L., attorney.
Hyde, H., boots and shoes.
Jacoby, B., clothing.
Jett, M. E., contractor and builder.
Jillson, R. B., dry goods.
Jones & Wright, woolen mill.
Kattenbrun, V., boots and shoes.
Kearsay, Silas, saddle and harness.
Kenne, Fred., toys and confectionery.
Kentucky Yeoman, S. I. M. Major, pub.
Kiernan, John, grocer.
Lindsay, T. N., pres't Farmers' Bank Kentucky.
Lindsey, T. N. & D. W., attorneys.
McClure, R. K. & Bro., boots, shoes, hats, caps, books, stationery, &c.
McConn, J. E., distiller.
McGill, A., prop'r Capitol Hotel.
McGrew, M., saw mill.
Macklin, G. B., lumber.
Major & Jett, attorneys.
Major, S. I. M., pub. Kentucky Yeoman.
Mangan & Walker, pottery.
Meek, B. F., watches, jewelry, and silver ware.
Milam, B., jewelry.
Miller, Henry, stoves and tin ware.
Miller, G. W., stoves and tin ware.
Mills, Dr. J. M., drugs, cigars, and fancy articles.
Moore, J. L. & Son, dry goods, carpets.
Murray, W. H. & Co., saw mill.
Neffner, N., merchant tailor.
Newman & Bro., grocers.
Newman & Welch, grocers.
Noel & Bacon, livery stable.
O'Donnell, James, boots and shoes.
O'Hara, Jas. P., hide and leather.
Owen, G. W., ag't Adams Express Co.
Peters, David, autioneer.
Power, Edmon, mfr tin, zinc, copper, and sheet iron ware, and dealer in stoves, grates, &c.
Rea & Burns, carriage and wagon mfrs.
Redding, Mrs. J. P. & Son, dry goods and notions.
Rodman, H., cotton mill.
Rodman & Bro., wholesale and retail dry goods, notions, &c.
Rodman, John & J. W., attorneys.
Runyan, R., dry goods.
Saffell, J. & J. M., distillers.
Short, Frank, carpenter and builder.
Steele & Gay, coal.
Stephens, Walker, wholesale and retail grocer.
Stoughton, Mrs. R., millinery.
Strowbridge, Mrs. E. C., millinery and fancy goods.
Sullivan, T. H., dry goods, &c.
Taylor, E. H., cash. Bank of Kentucky.
Tobin, L., retail grocer.
Todd, Jas. M., groceries and liquors.
Todd, H. J., lessee and keeper Kentucky Penitentiary and ware house.
Turner, W., dry goods.
Waggoner, J. L. & W. H., dry goods, hats, caps, &c.
Walaschek, L., undertaker and dealer in furniture.
Watson, J. R., prop'r Mansion House.
Watson, John, cashier Deposit Bank of Frankfort.
Weitzell, L., baker and confectioner.
Whitesides, Jno., carpenter & builder.
Williams, Henry, retail grocer.

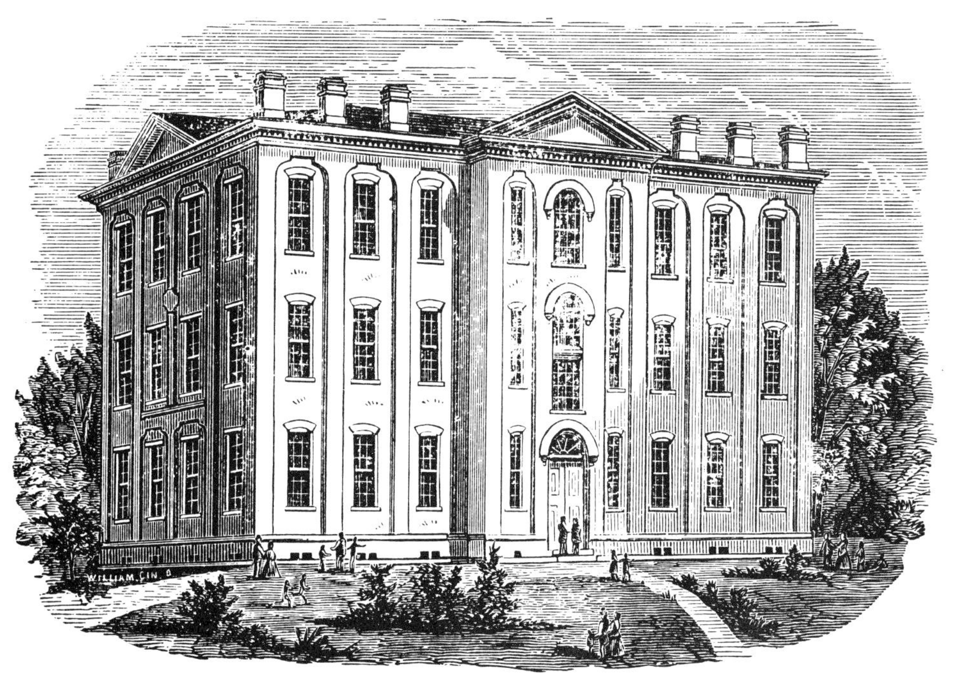

The actual high school building was rebuilt after a fire in the 1860s and became more ornate than depicted in this drawing from Collins' *History of Kentucky*. A cupola topped off with a weathervane is shown in the pre-1906 view. In order to accommodate an ever-increasing number of students, the front became the side, and wings were added. When a new Second Street School was constructed on the site of the old one, old school cornerstones were incorporated into the structure.

Courtesy of Western Kentucky University, Kentucky Library.

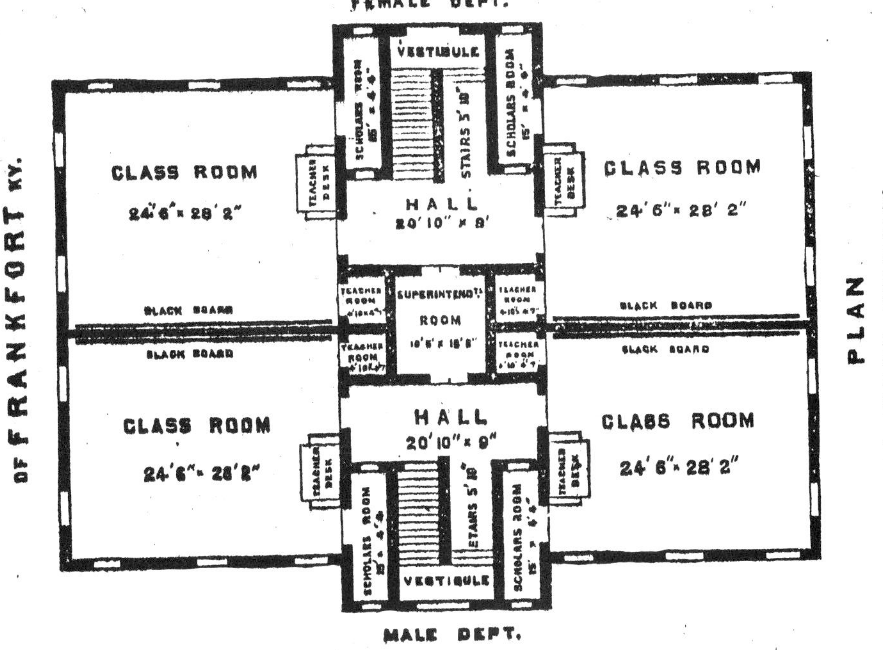

The Frankfort High School was featured in an 1876 book on Kentucky education, from which this floor plan is taken. There were separate male and female departments, and each sex entered the building from a different side.

From the Sprague Postcard Collection.

Kentucky.

Second Street, circa 1905. The Second Street School appears at the right with newly laid curbing and an iron fence. The large building on the left is now the Rogers Funeral Home. Photograph courtesy of Kentucky Historical Society.

A Frankfort High School graduating class at the turn of the century. The mustachioed man in the back row is the principal, Professor George Downing, a man of many talents. In addition to administering the school, he taught eight classes in 1901: solid geometry and conic sections, trigonometry, physical geography, physics, chemistry, physiology, civics, and college requirements. Photograph courtesy of Kentucky Historical Society.

In 1910 the Farmers Tobacco Warehouse Company built a large warehouse at 406-14 West Second Street, where the Second Street School playground is now. Across the street was located the Geary Tobacco Warehouse Company at 415-17 Second Street. The combined sales of the two warehouses in 1910 equalled 8½ million pounds. Photograph courtesy of Kentucky Historical Society.

Second Street, circa 1912, is the scene of a parade with an educational twist: the lead automobile sports a sign saying "Commercial"; the second car announces "Math." One is tempted to declare in the language of Sesame Street that this parade is brought to you by the letter "P". For a time the enlarged Second Street School housed all of Frankfort's scholars, kindergarten through grade twelve, and, by means of a contract with Franklin County, all of the county's high school students. City school enrollment figures for 1920 indicate that nearly one-third of the school children were in first or second grade, and less than fifteen percent were in grades nine through twelve. Photograph courtesy of Kentucky Historical Society.

This view shows *Summer Girl* in 1922, with the Second Street School in the background. The excursion boat was hired out for the Kentucky Bankers' Association outing. Photograph courtesy of University of Kentucky Postcard Collection.

Flood of February 1883

OPPOSITE
Top:
Crawfish Bottom—better known as The Craw. Photograph courtesy of Kentucky Historical Society.

Center:
Toward Bellepoint. Photograph courtesy of Kentucky Historical Society.

Bottom:
The Craw during the flood. Photograph courtesy of Kentucky Historical Society.

"Not in the recollection of the oldest inhabitant of Frankfort nor in either history or tradition was there any account of the waters of the Kentucky River ever having been so high as in February 1883. Nearly all the families in the lower part of the city were moved out. All of the section known as 'Craw' was completely covered. On Sunday night the 11th of February, a great many Frankfort people remained up all night, expecting to see the St. Clair bridge washed away. A heavy drfit was running and it began to accumulate above the piers. A large new tobacco barn struck the middle pier and its timbers were scattered in every direction .The upper sidewalk of the bridge was greatly damaged, the sides and floor for some distance were completely destroyed and much of the sheeting under the roof was torn away...

"The railroad bridge was considerably damaged by the drift and for some time it looked like it would be impossible to save it. A long freight train heavily loaded was left standing on it to help hold it. All the houses on Broadway and High Streets from the Farmers Hotel, east, were completely surrounded. More than a hundred houses passed under the St. Clair Street bridge, nearly all of which were torn to pieces." Johnson, *History of Franklin County, Kentucky.*

The magnitude of the flood can be seen by comparing this Mattern photograph of the wooden bridge with the 1883 photograph of the flood waters, which had risen to meet the roadway. The extensive damage to the center of the structure is cleary delineated. Photographs courtesy of Kentucky Historical Society.

Looking towards Second Street School. The school in this view is similar to the illustration in Collins' *History of Kentucky*. Photograph courtesy of Kentucky Historical Society.

Rodman and Sneed lumber yard during the 1883 flood. The 1882 Franklin County *Atlas* says of this steam saw and planning mill, owned by G.R. Rodman and J.L. Sneed: "Dealers in all kinds of Rough and Dressed Lumber. Manufacturers of Doors, Sash, Blinds, Moulding, Brackets, Stairs, and Builders' Finishing Material. Office at Mills, near R. R. Bridge. John L. Sneed & Co., Hardwood Lumber Dealers, Walnut, Poplar, Oak, &c. in Wholesale Lots at Lower Mill." Photograph courtesy of Kentucky Historical Society.

On August 10, 1883, E. J. Carpenter climbed the hill and took this view of the dam. Photograph courtesy of U.S. Army Corps of Engineers, Louisville District.

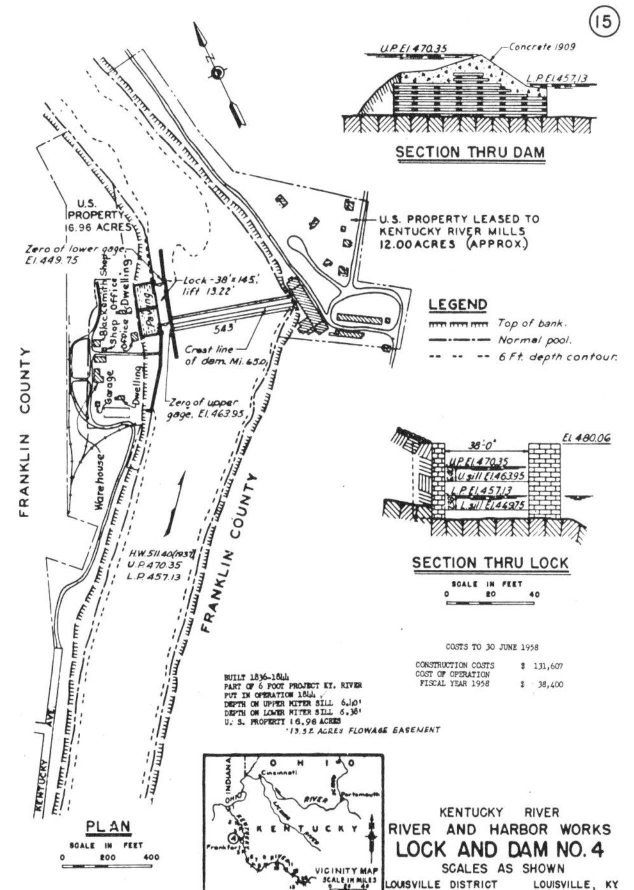

Lock #4 has been in operation since 1844 and has been remodeled since this 1958 diagram. Courtesy of Kentucky Historical Society.

This August 8, 1883, view of work on the wooden dam shows the Kentucky River Mills in the background. The firm manufactured hemp yarns and twines, with grain binding twine a specialty. Photograph courtesy of U.S. Army Corps of Engineers, Louisville District.

This card, postmarked March 17, 1906, predates the concrete paving of the dam. From the Sprague Postcard Collection.

These two views of the lock and dam were taken after 1909, when the concrete paving was added. From the Sprague Postcard Collection.

Steamboats were an integral part of the Frankfort scene for a century; by 1900 approximately two dozen of them plied the Kentucky River. During the summer, excursion boats would leave the Customs House wharf for a four-hour cruise to Lock #5 and back. From the Sprague Postcard Collection.

Steamboats pushing coal barges were once a common sight. Photograph courtesy of Kentucky Historical Society.

The 145½-foot U.S. towboat *General O. M. Poe* carried passengers and freight from Louisville to the headwaters of the Kentucky River, returning with passengers, produce, and livestock for the market. One long-time resident remembers that the 150-ton *Poe* made the biggest waves on the river. Photograph courtesy of Kentucky Historical Society.

The steamer *Falls City* was built in Cincinnati in 1899, burned the following year at the Seventh Street wharf in Louisville, was rebuilt in Jeffersonville, and entered the Kentucky River trade soon afterwards. The deck captain was Jonathan E. Abraham, the wheel captain J. J. Preston. In 1908 the ship was sold to Captain T. M. Morrissey of Vicksburg and entered the Mississippi River trade until 1915, when she was laid up and later dismantled. The schedule shows forty-two possible stops for the *Falls City* in Franklin County alone. Photograph and schedule courtesy of Kentucky Historical Society.

LOUISVILLE & KENTUCKY RIVER PACKET COMPANY INC.

MAIN OFFICE,
178
FOURTH AVENUE
Home Phone 135
LOUISVILLE, KENTUCKY

COMMERCE LINE
Operating
The Up-to-Date
Steamer

Falls City

Time Table Steamer Falls City, up stream; landings along Kentucky River, miles from Louisville, Ky., giving Counties in which landings are located.

Monday Trip, Leaving Louisville, Ky. 3:00 P. M., through to Valley View, Ky., arriving Wednesday, 5:30 A. M.
Friday Trip, Leaving Louisville, Ky. 3:00 P. M., through to Frankfort, Ky., only, arriving Saturday, noon.

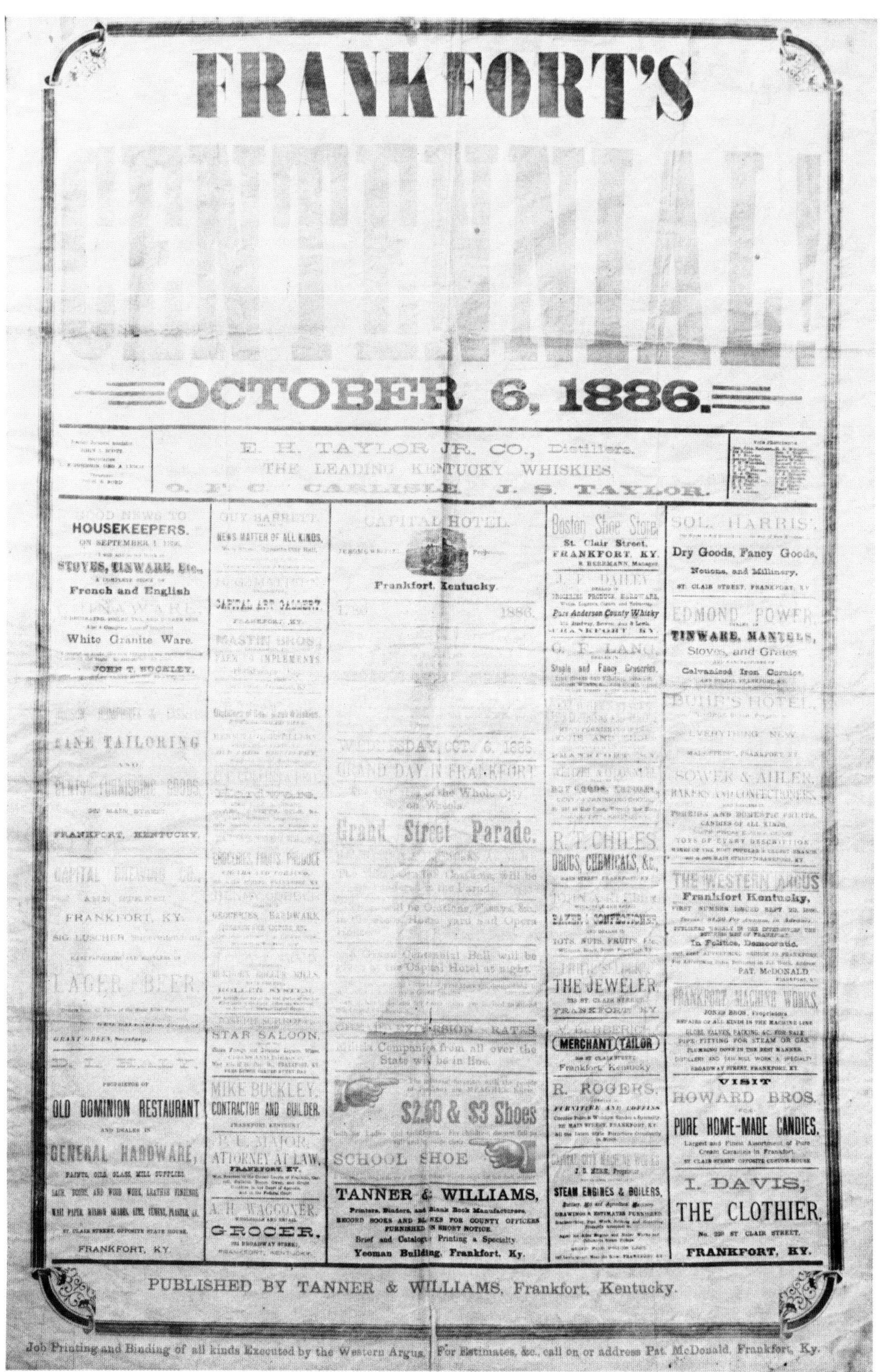

A handbill advertises the Frankfort Centennial which according to the Louisville *Courier-Journal*, was a grand success: "This is unquestionably the biggest day Frankfort has ever witnessed. The trains have been emptying their coaches so long at the depot that an observer is impressed with the belief that everybody and his cousin in Kentucky and adjoining states are here. The streets, both on the north and south sides, are impassable with pedestrians, and there is not a window or a balcony in the line of march, which takes in every street in the city, but has a group of beautiful faces set in ribbons and feathers. . . ." Handbill courtesy of Kentucky Historical Society.

Centennial

Canton Berry, No. 6, Independent Order of Odd Fellows, and The Blue Ribbon Gospel Temperance Mission Band, two of the groups marching in the Centennial Parade. Photograph courtesy of Kentucky Historical Society.

"To stand at the corner of Broadway and St. Clair Streets and look towards the depot, a sea of flags and bunting met the eye, and from the intersection of Main and St. Clair Streets the view met in either direction was entrancing."—*Frankfort Roundabout*, October 9, 1886. Photograph courtesy of Kentucky Historical Society.

"But by far the most charming sight of all was the countless number of beautiful women to be seen upon the sidewalks, in the windows and on the doorsteps as the procession moved through the streets in the morning," reported the *Frankfort Roundabout*, October 9, 1886. Photograph courtesy of Kentucky Historical Society.

"At 9½ o'clock the pupils of the white and colored Public Schools and Catholic School, numbering about 1,000 children, formed in procession, and headed by a band of Music, marched through the principal streets of the city, presenting a beautiful appearance," according to the *Frankfort Roundabout*, October 9, 1886. Photograph courtesy of Kentucky Historical Society.

Inaugurated] *[Feb 10th, 1878.*

"I can do all things through Christ which strengtheneth me."

PLEDGE CARD

OF

THE BLUE RIBBON

GOSPEL TEMPERANCE MISSION.

I, the undersigned, Promise by Divine Assistance to abstain from all Intoxicating Liquors as Beverages, and to Discountenance their use by others. Lord, help me, for Jesus' sake.

SIGNED ....

William Noble 188

Copyright.—Hoxton Hall (Headquarters of the Movement), Hoxton, London, N.

E. W. Partridge & Co. 9 Paternoster Row London E.C.

A Blue Ribbon pledge card. Courtesy of Kentucky Historical Society.

Simon Bolivar Buckner, governor 1889-91.

Judge Thomas H. Hines, delegate from Franklin County.

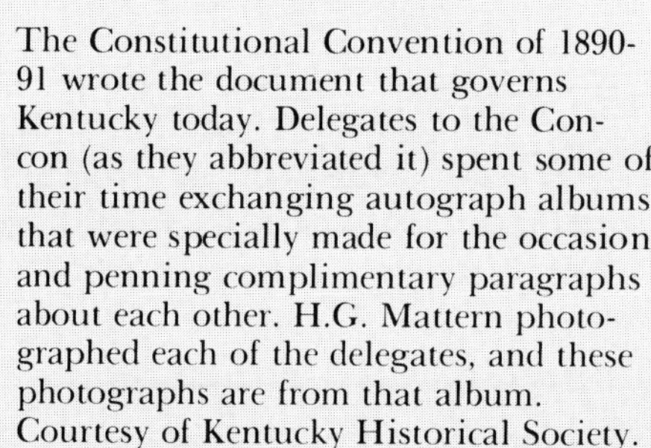

The Constitutional Convention of 1890-91 wrote the document that governs Kentucky today. Delegates to the Con-con (as they abbreviated it) spent some of their time exchanging autograph albums that were specially made for the occasion and penning complimentary paragraphs about each other. H.G. Mattern photographed each of the delegates, and these photographs are from that album. Courtesy of Kentucky Historical Society.

Cassius Marcellus Clay, Jr., convention chairman.

J. Proctor Knott, governor.

William Goebel, future governor.

"The State House columns were wrapped with bunting, and flags were distributed in profusion about the front of the building. The front fence was twined with evergreens, and the words 'Centennial Welcome,' in large letters of different colors, adorned the top."—*Frankfort Roundabout*, October 9, 1886. Photograph courtesy of Kentucky Historical Society.

The first office of the State National Bank, founded in 1889, was in the Hume Building, across the street from the Farmers Bank. The original officers were: Fayette Hewitt, president; H. P. Mason, vice-president; Charles E. Hoge, cashier; and F. V. Gray, assistant cashier. Photograph by Gretter; courtesy of Kentucky Historical Society.

The Post Office, designed and built by D. A. Murphy of Danville, opened in 1887. Both the top and bottom views were taken between that time and 1893, when the old wooden bridge was replaced. Courtesy of Kentucly Historical Society.

The covered bridge on St. Clair Street. After the Army Corps of Engineers took over the rivers, all bridges were ordered lifted to a specified height. The old wooden bridge was replaced in 1893 by the present Singing Bridge. Photograph courtesy of Kentucky Historical Society.

Courtesy of John E. Thierman Photograph Collection, Francis Carrick Thomas Library, Transylvania University.

Opposite:
A horse-drawn hearse of the type common around the turn of the century. Photograph courtesy of Kentucky Historical Society.

R. Rogers & Sons on St. Clair Street combined the businesses of undertaking and furniture making, a common practice in the nineteenth century. The building was built for the *Kentucky Yeoman*. The Frankfort Business College used this photograph and blocked in their name. Since the enterprise does not appear in city directories, one concludes it did not last long. Photograph courtesy of Kentucky Historical Society.

CRUTCHER & STARKS' Great Establis

MILAM'S FAMOUS FRANKFORT, KENTUCKY,
Fishing Reel.

They are made of Fine Silver, German Silver and Brass. With care, will last a lifetime.

They are always in order. Of the thousands that are now in use, not one has failed to give satis'a t on.

These Reels are absolutely perfect, both in workmanship and material. The first ones made are in true working order to-day. For catalogue and price list address the sole manufacturers,

B. C. MILAM & SON.

The 1879-80 City Directory contains an advertisement for Benjamin C. Milam (formerly Meek & Milam), manufacturer of fine silver, German silver, and brass fishing reels. Courtesy of Kentucky Historical Society.

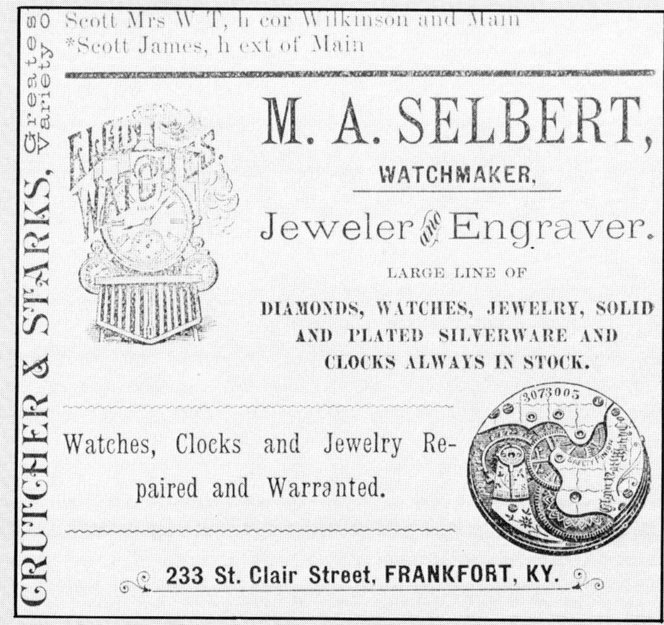

M. A. Selbert advertisement from the 1891 City Directory. The firm has been located on St. Clair Street since 1872. Courtesy of Kentucky Historical Society.

This view shows a streetcar coming across the St. Clair Street Bridge, which opened for traffic on March 24, 1894, a week before the electric railway was put into operation. Note the then-new YMCA building to the right, at 104 Bridge Street. In the background one can barely make out portions of the Hanna House. The advertising card in the interurban is for Fairy Soap. Photograph courtesy of Kentucky Historical Society.

On Wednesday, March 28, 1894, at 2:30 in the afternoon, the cars of Frankfort's new electric railway were brought out, filled with prominent citizens, and taken over the loop on the South Side. The cars were then all run out on Main Street, where they were photographed by H. G. Mattern. This view of car 19 by Gretter was taken in 1911. Photograph courtesy of Kentucky Historical Society.

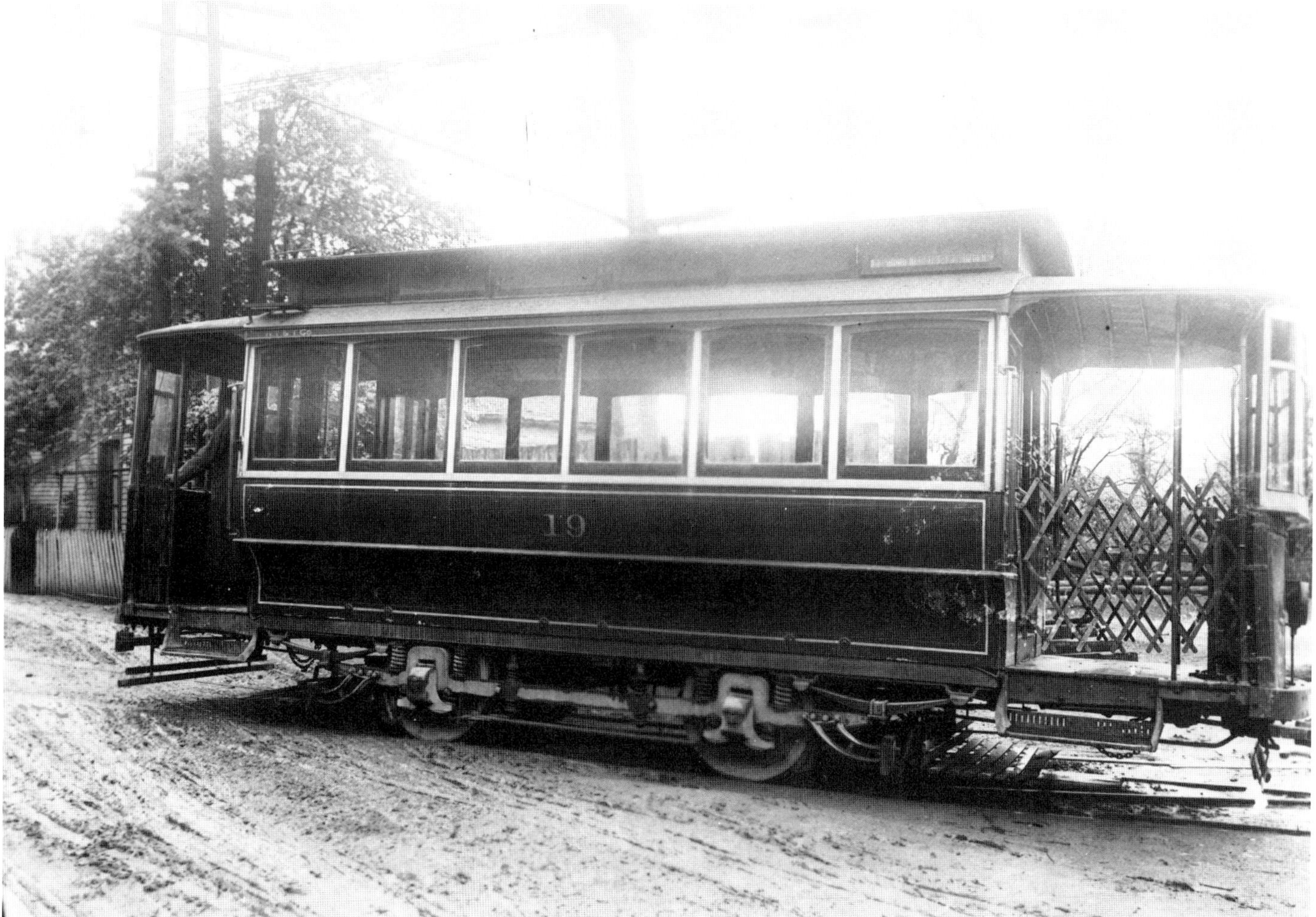

This view shows the new (1894) St. Clair Street Bridge. The Terraces, the colonnaded residence to the left of the Customs House/Post Office, is prominent, as is the wing of the State House, to the right of the old Capitol. The Capitol Hotel, the Court House, and the Penitentiary, as well as a variety of churches, are in the picture. Photograph courtesy of Kentucky Historical Society.

Company E, Second Regiment, Kentucky Volunteers, known as the Bradley Guards, was among the group of soldiers from Franklin County that fought in the Spanish-American War. Photograph courtesy of Kentucky Historical Society.

The Capitol Hotel, whose architect, Isiah Rogers, has been called the father of the modern hotel, designed this landmark in 1852. It was ready for occupancy by the time the legislature met in late 1853. Other famous Rogers' hotels include the second Galt House in Louisville and the Burnet House in Cincinnati. This view was taken during the Centennial parade. Photograph courtesy of Kentucky Historical Society.

A sheet of Capital Hotel stationery. Courtesy of Kentucky Historical Society.

The Capital Hotel ballroom was the scene of many glittering social events. This dance card for the Mardi Gras Ball in 1876 listed twenty-one dances, including the quadrille, galop, lancers, polka redowa, and waltz. At this time the original spelling Capitol Hotel had been changed to Capital. Courtesy of Kentucky Historical Society.

The flood of August 1899 was minor by Frankfort standards, except to those the waters reached. Photograph courtesy of University of Kentucky Postcard Collection.

This postcard is derived from a photograph that shows a streetlight over the cupola and tree branches in the upper left corner. Such a photograph was made into a postcard without retouching. The American News Company postcard eliminated the bulb and twigs. When Goebel was assassinated, the same view was used, but a funeral crowd brushed in with a portrait of Goebel in an oval added to the upper left corner. The Souvenir Post Card Company retouched the original photograph, causing the disappearance of telephone poles (except for one to the right of the hotel) and instant foliage on the leafless trees. Both cards are postmarked 1906. From the Sprague Postcard Collection.

The Capitol Hotel aged gracefully, as this circa 1912 view shows. Photograph courtesy of Kentucky Historical Society.

This double postcard was made in the early days of the twentieth century after the introduction of the streetcar and before the replacement of multi-tiered telephone poles. Courtesy of University of Kentucky, Miscellaneous Postcard Collection.

Disaster struck on April 5, 1917, when fire ravaged the Capitol Hotel. But just as this hotel has risen on the site of the Weisiger House, so the location remained prime, and the old landmark was replaced by the new Capitol Hotel. Photograph by Gretter; courtesy of Kentucky Historical Society.

Paul Sawyier's rendition of the Wapping Street Fountain, one of those amenities of urban life that has disappeared. Photograph of painting courtesy of Kentucky Historical Society.

Paul Sawyier and Mary Thomas Bull, circa 1900. Their romance has been the cause of much speculation: although apparently engaged for some time, neither ever married. From a photograph owned by J. J. King of Frankfort; courtesy of Kentucky Historical Society.

The family of the artist Paul Sawyier was photographed outside The Studio at 424 Broadway, in the fall of 1886. *Back row, left to right:* Henry Wingate Sawyier, Penelope Hart Wingate, Maria L. Campbell, Dr. Nathaniel J. Sawyier, Jr., Ellen Wingate Sawyier, Paul Sawyier; *front row:* Lilian Sawyier (Hill), Mary Campbell Sawyier (Neiss-Waner), and Natalie Sawyier (Bentz). Photograph from the Wingate/Sawyier scrapbook; courtesy of Kentucky Historical Society.

Hazelrigg's stable was located at 321 West Main Street, where the State Journal Building is now. Photograph by Gretter; courtesy of Kentucky Historical Society.

Interesting patterns of wallpaper are revealed as the future site of the McClure Building is prepared. To the left can be seen C. C. Hazelrigg's Livery. Photograph courtesy of Kentucky Historical Society.

The Frankfort Fire Department was located on Main Street from at least 1882. John C. Fuss remembers that the steam engine was drawn by "two beautiful white horses," who may be the same ones as shown in this view. He also recalls that the hook and ladder wagon was drawn by one big sorrel horse named Frank. A bell mounted on the top of the firehouse rang the number of strokes signalling the ward in which the alarm was given. In 1912 the department had one hose wagon, one hook and ladder and three horses. Photograph courtesy of Kentucky Historical Society.

Opposite Page:

Cadet Noel Jones in 1905. In 1843 Colonel R. T. P. Allen founded the Kentucky Military Institute, to be run by the same methods as West Point. The location he chose was the once-popular health resort Franklin Springs on Lawrenceburg Road. In 1893 Dr. John Stuart bought the property to start a school for retarded children. It is still run as a home for the mentally retarded. Photograph courtesy of Kentucky Historical Society.

Lynch's Monuments was located on Broadway on the slope leading to the Arsenal. Photograph courtesy of Kentucky Historical Society.

The seven-story McClure Building at Main and St. Clair streets was Frankfort's first skyscraper, built for the McClure Realty Company. Courtesy of University of Kentucky Postcard Collection.

The ladies' suit department at McClure's. Courtesy of University of Kentucky Postcard Collection.

K.M.I.
K.M.I.

A rude bungalow served the citizenry of the capital city as a country club. From the Sprague Postcard Collection.

Trap shooting in Frankfort, circa 1900. Note the formality of the costumes. The fourth man from the right is George Darsie, pastor of the First Christian Church; to his left is George L. Payne, an insurance agent. Photograph courtesy of Kentucky Historical Society.

Dr. C. K. Wallace was a prominent Frankfort physician with offices in the Baxter Building. In this photograph by Wolff he also displays a taste for theatre. Courtesy of Kentucky Historical Society.

The FRANKFORT CHAIR CO.

FRANKFORT, KY.

MANUFACTURERS OF

CHAIRS

OF ALL KINDS

Goods Sold to the Trade Only

All Local Dealers Handle Our Goods

Several trades were practiced in the reformatory, including the manufacture of rugs, shoes, shirts, and chairs. Inmates (some wearing striped pants) are shown at the chair factory. The advertisement offers Penitentiary-built chairs. Photograph and advertisement courtesy of Kentucky Historical Society.

Segregated inmates pose for their photograph, circa 1900. Most appear to be young men. Photograph by Wolff; courtesy of Kentucky Historical Society.

Compare this view of the Penitentiary grounds with the 1937 flood view. Photograph courtesy of Kentucky Historical Society.

A general view of the Penitentiary grounds. Note the entrance towers, *right*. Courtesy of University of Kentucky Postcard Collection.

William Goebel

William Goebel was one of those politicians whose stands and methods made him a predictable target for assassination. To his enemies he was a power-hungry city boss from Covington, a demagogue who used the Louisville and Nashville Railroad as an issue to curry favor with the common man. He was somewhat of a crowd pleaser, but an abject failure when it came to talking to voters one on one. He was ruthless and was known to stab allies in the back. Goebel was to his friends the best-informed politician in the state, a friend to the poor, to the farmer, to labor.

The gubernatorial campaign of 1899 was one of the bitterest in Kentucky's history. It should have been a Democratic year but an acrimonious and underhanded convention fight cut his strength. Goebel allied himself with William J. Stone, another gubernatorial hopeful, to defeat "Wat" Hardin. But once this was achieved, Goebel refused to withdraw, though he had promised to do so. Goebel barely won the nomination. The "Kenton Czar" had additional liabilities. He had gunned down John L. Sanford, a political opponent in April 1895, in—to put the best face on it—a near instantaneous duel. Goebel favored the gold standard until 1896, then came out for Free Silver. In 1898 he rammed through the Election Law that bears his name, making it possible for the party in power to select the governor in close elections. Trickster, charlatan, and dictator were among the descriptors, used by his enemies to modify the word Goebel. The Kenton County Democrat's style was such that he did not unite his party but rather, pugnaciously struck out at the power Louisville and Nashville Railroad. The L & N was not backward in involving itself in state politics, but the vitriolic onslaught forced the line to back Republican William S. Taylor with greater financial support than was customary.

Both sides expected the other would use fraud and force to win. Both sides brought in their heavy artillery. William Jennings Bryan, who had lost the state by a scant 281 votes in 1896, swung through the state in mid-October and the Republicans countered with their Governor, "Billy O. B." (William O. Bradley).

William Goebel, campaigning against the Louisville and Nashville Railroad and Republican William S. Taylor. Photograph courtesy of Kentucky Historical Society.

With predictions of treachery, Republican William S. Taylor's victory by fewer than 2,400 votes out of approximately 400,000 assured controversy. Democrats claimed fraud existed in fully one-third of the state's counties. Two committees were chosen by lot to investigate the election of the governor and lieutenant governor. When in each case nine of the eleven turned out to be Republicans, there were additional outcries of fraud.

Soon the word went out and armed Republican sympathizers arrived

This turn-of-the-century view is the earliest that has been located of a long line of photographs looking down St. Clair Street toward the old Capitol. From the Sprague Postcard Collection.

Goebel's assassination triggered a bitter partisan dispute. In this photograph by E. Carl Wolff, Kentucky State Guardsmen man a Gatling gun in front of the old Capitol annex. Photograph courtesy of Kentucky Historical Society.

in large numbers. An already unstable situation became even more critical. No matter what the election commission decided, there was a good chance it would lead to violence by the defeated party.

Goebel left his chamber at the Capitol Hotel on the morning of January 30, 1900, and arrived on the Capitol grounds. A shot rang out and Goebel fell, mortally wounded. He was brought back to the Capitol Hotel, where he lingered for a hundred hours. In the interim, he was sworn in as Governor. The coming of the Louisville Legion and the Second Regiment brought some relief to the situation. Goebel died February 3, 1900, and his body was viewed by 100,000 at Saint Paul's German Protestant Church in Covington. Then avoiding the L & N, the body was brought back by a circuitous route over the track of the Queen & Crescent line to Frankfort. His casket lay in the Capitol Hotel before being brought to the Frankfort cemetery for burial. Assassination insured that Goebel would not be forgotten, and his final words, reported by a Democrat, "tell my friends to be brave, fearless, and loyal to the great common people," helped make him a folk hero. Politics has been defined as the art of compromise, but Goebel was uncompromising to the end.

This 1912 view of the lobby is the only known interior photograph of the old Capitol Hotel. An illustration in the Louisville *Courier-Journal* of January 17, 1900, assures us that there is little difference between the lobby at the time of the Goebel assassination and this view. On January 16, 1900, William Jennings Bryan arrived to help support Goebel. The Great Commoner was met by a crowd of a thousand despite the rain, and rode in a handsome carriage in company with the newly selected United States Senator "Old Jo" Blackburn, William Goebel, and Speaker Trimble. At nine o'clock an informal reception was held in the Capitol Hotel.

Earlier in the day the famed hostelry had been the scene of a personal vendetta that left three dead and four wounded. Among those who escaped unscathed were ex-Governor James B. McCreary and County Attorney James Polsgrove. Politicians were gathering from all parts of the Commonwealth to see the contested election through. Photograph courtesy of Kentucky Historical Society.

Protected from the January cold by caped greatcoats, State Guardsmen patrol a tense capital city. Armed factions threatened violence for weeks after Goebel's death. Photograph by Wolff; courtesy of Kentucky Historical Society.

A detachment of guardsmen stand at attention on Broadway. Photograph by Wolff; courtesy of Kentucky Historical Society.

J. C. W. Beckham, lieutenant governor, took the oath of office at Goebel's deathbed. After the Republican candidate, W. S. Taylor, fled the city, Beckham assumed office; he was elected to his own term in 1903. Photograph courtesy of Kentucky Historical Society.

The Court House is still decorated with signs of mourning and a guardsman keeps an eye on the situation, shouldering his rifle with bayonet attached. Photograph by Wolff; courtesy of Kentucky Historical Society.

During the Goebel crisis Frankfort was threatened by a miniature civil war as each party attempted to control the State House. Bayonet-armed guardsmen blocked the entrance to the Capitol grounds. Photograph by Wolff; courtesy of Kentucky Historical Society.

The squat building to the left of the old Capitol was razed in 1912. It housed the Auditor's and Treasurer's Office, but with the building of the new Capitol, the structure was deemed unnecessary. Photograph courtesy of University of Kentucky Nollan Collection.

This turn-of-the-century postcard shows Main Street, looking east. From the Sprague Postcard Collection.

The most common early postcard view of Frankfort. Note the billboards on thefar shore under the bridge, characteristic of early twentieth century cityscapes. From the Sprague Postcard Collection.

The Bibb House. Photograph by W. B. Oelza; courtesy of Kentucky Historical Society.

The Letcher-Lindsay House at 200 Washington Street, just a block from the present Paul Sawyier Library, was the old public library and is now the Frankfort Woman's Club. Photograph courtesy of Kentucky Historical Society.

The Robert P. Pepper house. Photograph courtesy of Kentucky Historical Society.

The South Frankfort Presbyterian Church was organized in 1884, and a frame structure was erected that year. A new building, shown here, was dedicated in 1904. The present minister is John L. Hunt. Courtesy of University of Kentucky Postcard Collection.

A turn-of-the-century view of Second Street, South Frankfort. Postcard courtesy of Kentucky Library, Western Kentucky University.

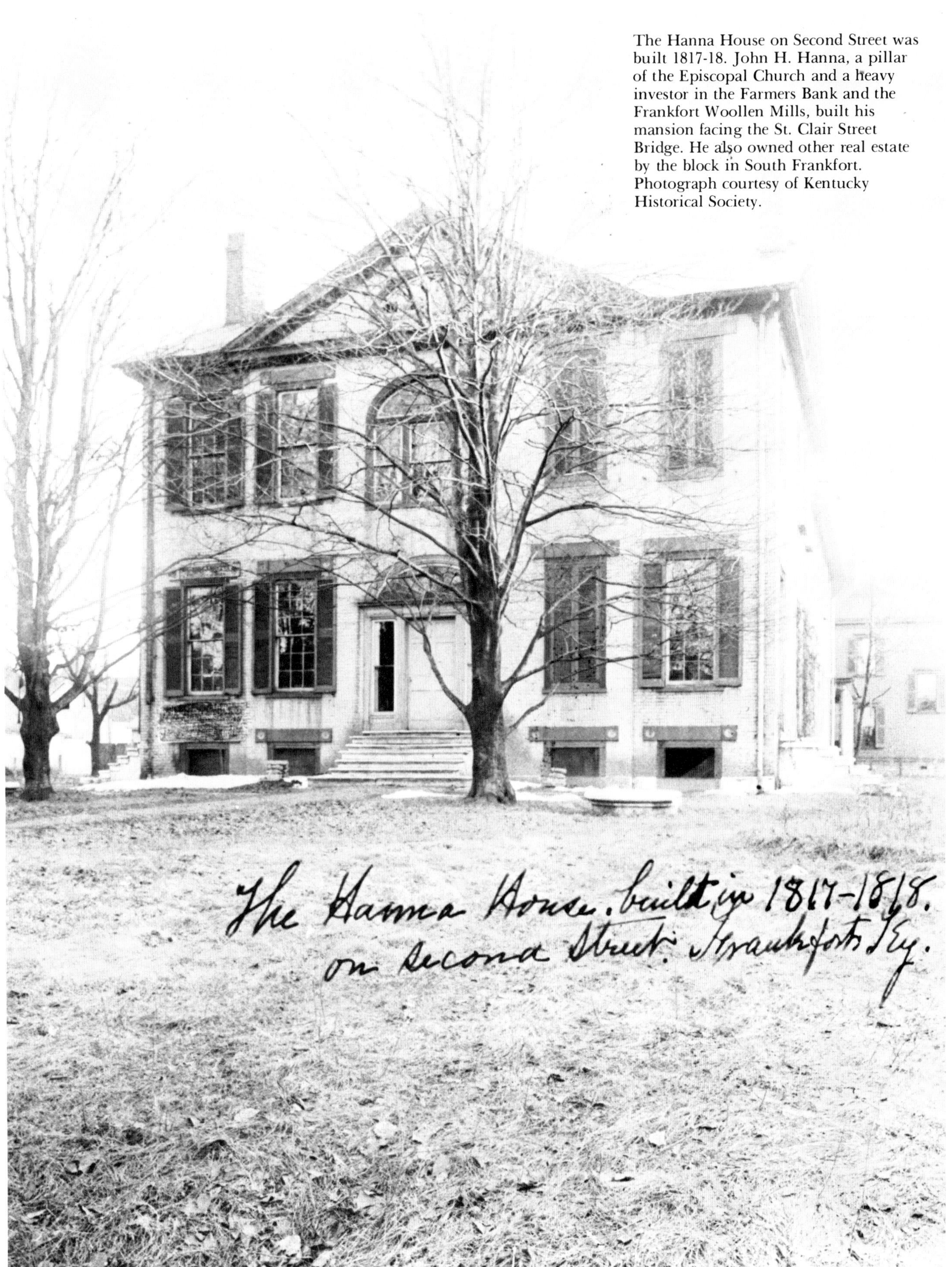

The Hanna House on Second Street was built 1817-18. John H. Hanna, a pillar of the Episcopal Church and a heavy investor in the Farmers Bank and the Frankfort Woollen Mills, built his mansion facing the St. Clair Street Bridge. He also owned other real estate by the block in South Frankfort. Photograph courtesy of Kentucky Historical Society.

The residence of George A. Lewis, editor of the *Frankfort Roundabout*, at 516 Cross Street in South Frankfort. Photograph by Mattern; courtesy of Kentucky Historical Society.

Daniel Weisiger Lindsey was city attorney of Frankfort prior to the Civil War. The roofing and ornamentation of his residence hide its pre-1820 construction date. Photograph courtesy of Kentucky Historical Society.

The Judge J. P. Hobson House, built 1833. Photograph courtesy of Kentucky Historical Society.

King's Daughters Hospital was founded by King's Daughters Silent Workers Circle—a group organized in 1894 as an outgrowth of the Chautauqua Movement, a national educational/lecture group operating out of Chatauqua, New York. The first hospital was opened in July 1896, and the second was located on Main Street and opened in 1938; an addition was constructed in 1956. The New King's Daughters Hospital, run by the Hospital Corporation of America, is named for the earlier group but not affiliated with it. The Circle is still active in Frankfort and plans to reopen the old hospital as apartments for the elderly.

Courtesy of University of Kentucky Postcard Collection.

Courtesy of Kentucky Historical Society.

In addition to managing his lumber company, Green Lyons built the Southern Hotel and many houses in South Frankfort, including those on Lyons Court. Photograph courtesy of Kentucky Historical Society.

An interior view of Strassner's house as it appeared in 1912. Photograph by Gretter; courtesy of Kentucky Historical Society.

In 1907 Charles Strassner completed his new residence at the corner of Todd and Shelby Streets in South Frankfort. His building material was "bird's-eye limestone," or "Kentucky River Marble," the same stone used in the old State Capitol, the old Capitol Hotel, and the old Farmer's Bank. Several quarries have operated in the county at various times. The exterior in 1979 is virtually unchanged. A small iron fence now graces the front, an air conditioning unit has been added and the mailbox moved across the street. Photograph by Cusick; courtesy of Kentucky Historical Society.

WAR SETTLEMENT WARRANT.

UNITED STATES TREASURY DEPARTMENT

No 5646

To the Treasurer of the United States, Washington, D.C. 1903

Pay to

or order

Dollars $

The

CERTIFICATE

No 20759

WILL PAY THIS WARRANT.

ASSISTANT TREASURER

ASSISTANT SECRETARY

COMPTROLLER

CHIEF CLERK

NOT OVER TWO MILLION DOLLARS

This 1903 U.S. Treasury War settlement warrant, made out to the governor of Kentucky in the amount of $1,317,778.71, was used to fund the new Capitol building. Warrant courtesy of Kentucky Historical Society.

The John Edward Glenn family, circa 1900. Glenn was the proprietor of the Frankfort Marble Works until he went into the grocery business. Glenn's Grocery, on the corner of Steele and Todd Streets in South Frankfort, is now the location of Sweasy's Market. Photograph and advertisement courtesy of Kentucky Historical Society.

HELLO! Phone E. T. 157 F. 226 .For Your Groceries

"Freshest, Purest, Best"
Cor. Steele and Todd

GLENN, the GROCER

The New Capitol

Approximately twenty thousand people attended the laying of the cornerstone for the new Capitol, June 16, 1906. The old Capitol was too small for modern use. Nationally, the functions of state government expanded greatly between 1865 and 1910. Moreover, Kentucky pride was at stake: America was engaged in a spate of Capitol-building, and Kentuckians did not want to appear backward. The architect was Frank Mills Andrews of Dayton, Ohio. Photograph by Cusick; courtesy of Kentucky Historical Society.

Progress photographs of construction of the new Capitol. Courtesy of Kentucky Historical Society.

Construction of the pediment at the new Capitol. Photograph courtesy of Kentucky Historical Society.

Construction crews at the new state Capitol. Photographs courtesy of Kentucky Historical Society.

The new Capitol with the Executive Mansion in the background. Photograph courtesy of Kentucky Historical Society.

The new Capitol provided adequate space for various branches of the state government. From the Sprague Postcard Collection.

The Executive Mansion remains the Governor's residence with rooms for public functions. Governor James B. McCreary (1911-1915) was the first resident of the mansion. Photograph courtesy of Kentucky Historical Society.

Ben L. Bruner, Secretary of State, and his stenographer, Minnie Lee McDaniel, were the first people to occupy their offices in the new state Capitol, moving in some seven weeks before any other officials. In this view, a lucky horseshoe hangs from their chandelier. Photograph by Gretter; courtesy of Kentucky Historical Society.

The 1908 legislative session was the last one held in the old Capitol. Photograph courtesy of Kentucky Historical Society.

The building of the new Capitol in South Frankfort led to renewed interest in development of this section. The new YMCA appears next to the St. Clair Street Bridge. Continuing towards the foreground on the same side of Second Street, one can see the Second Street School. Opposite the school is the building that has become the Rogers Funeral Home, and the large building on its right on Second became Vaughan's Garage. There is a tradition that the building was a skating rink at one time.

Piled-up lumber is an indication of a South Frankfort building boom, the result of the construction of the new Capitol.

Father Thomas Major was appointed pastor of the Church of the Good Shepherd in 1895, where he served until his death in 1911. Father Major was a Confederate soldier who converted to Catholicism during the war after falling sick and being nursed by nuns. Photograph by Gretter, 1907; courtesy of Kentucky Historical Society.

Opposite Top:
The Baptist Church on St. Clair Street. Photograph courtesy of Kentucky Historical Society.

An Episcopal Conference was held in 1906 at the Church of the Ascension. The church was built and furnished in 1850 by John H. Hanna, the first president of Farmers Bank. It is reported that Hanna went to Europe expressly to study Gothic architecture for use in the church building plans. Photograph by Gretter; courtesy of Kentucky Historical Society.

The 1911 Christian Church Convention included a display of religious publications and communion services. Photograph by Gretter; courtesy of Kentucky Historical Society.

First Baptist Choir in 1906. Photograph by Gretter; courtesy of Kentucky Historical Society.

Grace A.M.E. Church Choir in 1907. The conditions under which Frankfort's black citizens lived were those characteristic of Southern towns. Although living in close proximity, blacks and whites were separated by segregated churches, schools, and clubs. Blacks in Frankfort supported fraternal, literary, and cultural societies, as well as active church congregations. But the limitations of being black in Frankfort were clear. Johnson writes in his *History:* "During the half century which the negro has been free, not one of them has ever been tried in Franklin County by a legally constituted court for criminal assault (against a white), and doubtless during the next half century not one of them will be so tried." Photograph by Gretter; courtesy of Kentucky Historical Society.

The class of 1910. Photograph courtesy of Kentucky Historical Society.

Kentucky State University

The experimental farm of the agricultural department. Photograph by Gretter; courtesy of Kentucky Historical Society.

The State Normal School for Colored Persons was established by an 1887 act of the legislature to prepare teachers for the black public schools of Kentucky. The city council donated the sum of 1,500 dollars and the site which overlooks the city. In 1890 departments of agriculture, mechanics, and domestic economy were added. The legislature of 1904-06 appropriated twenty thousand dollars for new buildings, and further new construction followed the Second World War. Today the school is Kentucky State University, a racially integrated undergraduate and graduate institution with an enrollment of about 2,300.

Lettering class, 1911. Photograph by Gretter; courtesy of Kentucky Historical Society.

Domestic economy class in 1911. Photograph by Gretter; courtesy of Kentucky Historical Society.

Jackson Hall (1887) is the original building of what was then called the State Normal School for Colored Persons. Photograph by Stuart Sprague, April 1979.

New construction followed World War II. The Science Building is shown in July 1952. Photograph courtesy of J. Winston Coleman Kentuckiana Collection, Frances Carrick Thomas Library, Transylvania University.

In 1910 this building was completed, following the legislative appropriation of 1904-06. Photograph by Gretter; courtesy of Kentucky Historical Society.

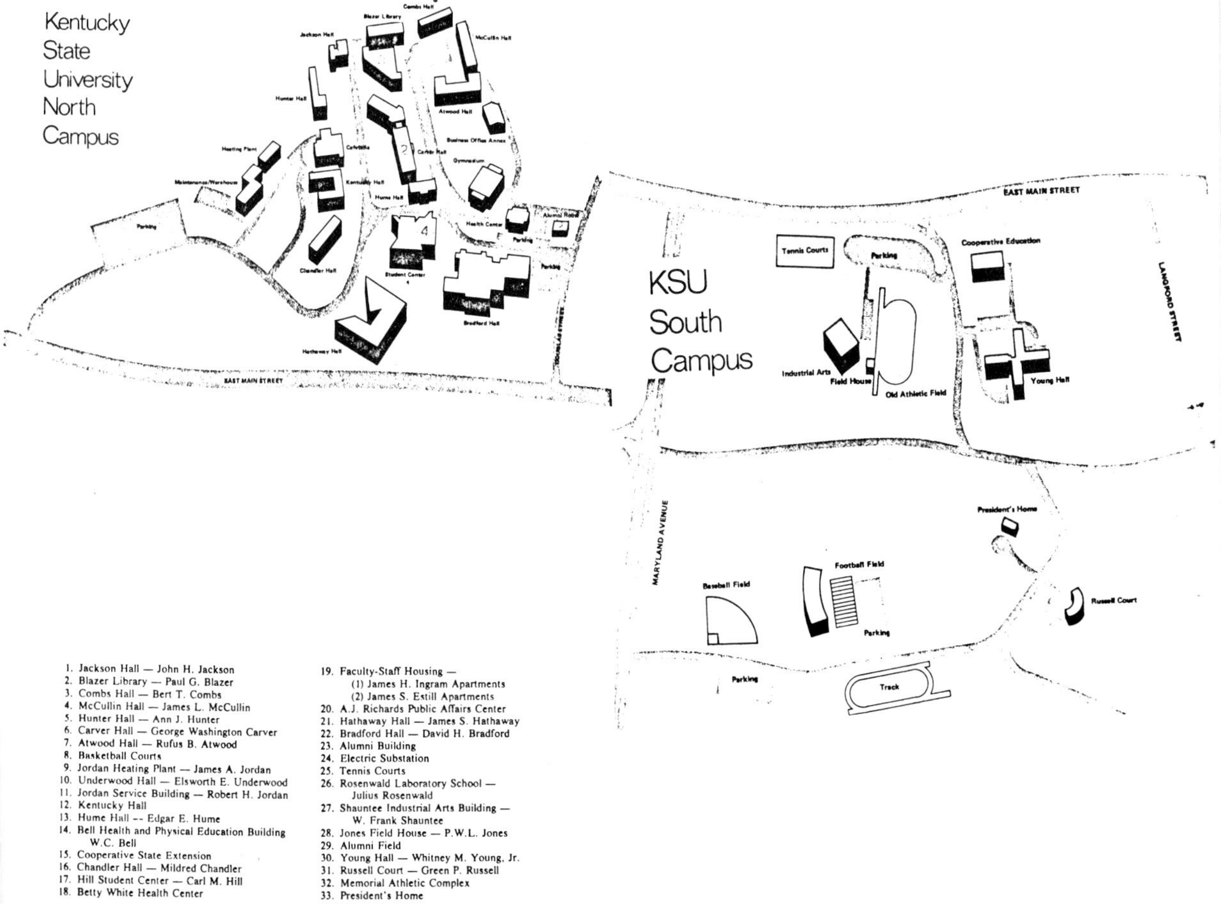

Kentucky State University North Campus

Combs Hall
Blazer Library
Jackson Hall
McCullin Hall
Hunter Hall
Atwood Hall
Business Office Annex
Heating Plant
Cafeteria
Carver Hall
Gymnasium
Maintenance/Warehouse
Kentucky Hall
Hume Hall
Parking
Health Center
Alumni Room
Chandler Hall
Student Center
Bradford Hall
Hathaway Hall
EAST MAIN STREET

KSU South Campus

EAST MAIN STREET
Tennis Courts
Parking
Cooperative Education
LANGFORD STREET
Industrial Arts
Field House
Old Athletic Field
Young Hall
MARYLAND AVENUE
President's Home
Football Field
Baseball Field
Russell Court
Parking
Parking
Track

1. Jackson Hall — John H. Jackson
2. Blazer Library — Paul G. Blazer
3. Combs Hall — Bert T. Combs
4. McCullin Hall — James L. McCullin
5. Hunter Hall — Ann J. Hunter
6. Carver Hall — George Washington Carver
7. Atwood Hall — Rufus B. Atwood
8. Basketball Courts
9. Jordan Heating Plant — James A. Jordan
10. Underwood Hall — Elsworth E. Underwood
11. Jordan Service Building — Robert H. Jordan
12. Kentucky Hall
13. Hume Hall -- Edgar E. Hume
14. Bell Health and Physical Education Building W.C. Bell
15. Cooperative State Extension
16. Chandler Hall — Mildred Chandler
17. Hill Student Center — Carl M. Hill
18. Betty White Health Center
19. Faculty-Staff Housing —
    (1) James H. Ingram Apartments
    (2) James S. Estill Apartments
20. A.J. Richards Public Affairs Center
21. Hathaway Hall — James S. Hathaway
22. Bradford Hall — David H. Bradford
23. Alumni Building
24. Electric Substation
25. Tennis Courts
26. Rosenwald Laboratory School — Julius Rosenwald
27. Shauntee Industrial Arts Building — W. Frank Shauntee
28. Jones Field House — P.W.L. Jones
29. Alumni Field
30. Young Hall — Whitney M. Young, Jr.
31. Russell Court — Green P. Russell
32. Memorial Athletic Complex
33. President's Home

Carver Hall, named after George Washington Carver, now has neighbors, including the Blazer Library. Photograph by Stuart Sprague, April 1979.

This view catches a corner of Hathaway Hall, which was named after James S. Hathaway, in the foreground. The Hill Student Center, named for Carl M. Hill, occupies the middle ground, while the Administration Building, Hume Hall, is the stone structure in the background. Photograph by Stuart Sprague, April 1979.

Holmes Street and the Penitentiary wall. The boundary of the city is clearly delineated from farm acreage in this photograph, taken before a highway system blurred such distinctions and provided us with a new term, "rurban." Photograph courtesy of Kentucky Historical Society.

The Tobin-Wathen bridal party in 1907 displays the latest in elegant Edwardian fashion. Photograph by Gretter; courtesy of Kentucky Historical Society.

Miss L. C. Berkhart models a very elegant costume in 1906. A city directory for this period lists five millinery shops, including Mrs. Watson's on St. Clair Street. Photograph by Gretter; courtesy of Kentucky Historical Society.

Kagin and Brothers Dry Goods, 105-07 St. Clair Street, circa 1910. Photograph by Gretter; courtesy of Kentucky Historical Society.

Harry A. Gretter, *front*, was Frankfort's photographer from 1902 to 1920. Here he takes his own photograph with the aid of a timer. Mrs. Gretter is standing, *center*. Photograph courtesy of Kentucky Historical Society.

Harry A. Gretter's car, parked in front of his studio in 1915, offers a solution for "a simple gift that lends the touch of friendship without the embarrassment of an obligation." Salender's saloon (109 St. Clair Street) can be seen next door. Photograph by Gretter; courtesy of Kentucky Historical Society.

In 1908 the Bluegrass Grocery Company was located on St. Clair Street, next to R. Rogers and Sons. Photograph by Gretter; courtesy of Kentucky Historical Society.

The imposing gentleman in the doorway of the Star Saloon is Gustave La Fontaine Schlegel, "Frenchy," proprietor of the Saratoga Refreshment Palace on St. Clair Street. Frenchy's nickname was attributed to his birth in Paris, France. Photograph by Wolff; courtesy of Kentucky Historical Society.

St. Clair Street, circa 1906: the names of the stores have changed over the years, but not the buildings. Since 1880 with the Frankfort Drug Store, there has been a corner drug store on St. Clair Street. On the right side of the street can be seen C. E. Collins Hardware, the M. A. Selbert clock, and the McClure Building under construction. Photograph courtesy of Kentucky Historical Society.

Harvey Wash's grocery (formerly Guthrie and Wash), 309 West Broadway, in 1910. His advertisements read: "fancy groceries, oysters, celery, etc." Photograph by Gretter; courtesy of Kentucky Historical Society.

The west portal of the railway tunnel, photographed in May 1939. Photograph courtesy of George H. Yater.

The train depot in 1974, shortly before the platform was removed. Freight trains still rumble through Frankfort, but passenger service ceased with the end of the George Washington, which ran from Louisville to Washington, D.C. Photograph courtesy of Kentucky Historical Society.

The Louisville and Nashville's "umbrella shed" was completed early in 1908, as was the building. Curiously enough, 1910 is the traditionally accepted date for the structure. The building has been recycled as the headquarters of the Kentucky Association of Highway Contractors, which had for forty years been located in the Capitol Hotel. Courtesy of University of Kentucky Postcard Collection.

A Main Street crowd waits in the rain for the posting of election returns, circa 1916. The McClure Building is visible in the background. Photograph courtesy of Kentucky Historical Society.

William Jennings Bryan climaxed his eleven-stop Kentucky tour on behalf of the YMCA on April 25, 1911. He arrived on the 10:20 train and was met by Mayor Polsgrove, ex-governor Beckham, and George C. Shaw. Bryan was driven to the YMCA site at 104 Bridge Street in Shaw's automobile. Augustus E. Willson, Kentucky's Republican governor, introduced the former Democratic standard bearer. Bryan quipped, regarding the YMCA, "You can realize what a strong tie it is when it holds Governor Willson and me on the same platform." When, during his forty-minute speech, Bryan declared that the YMCA was "about the only thing I know that has come to this country, that did not come through the customhouse," the crowd, estimated at 1,200, roared its approval. Robert L. Greene, president of the YMCA, assisted by C. Steele Reading, heading the local chapter of the Masons, laid the cornerstone. Once the ceremony was over, Bryan and his party visited the Elks home before boarding the 2 P.M. train. Two days later Bryan returned to Frankfort to deliver his "The Prince of Peace" lecture at the Capital Theatre, a benefit for the YMCA. A poster advertising the event is visible to the left of the bridge. Photograph by Gretter; courtesy of Kentucky Historical Society.

Y. M. C. A. Building, Frankfort, Ky.

The Chautauqua movement provided public lectures, concerts, and entertainment for the citizens of Frankfort. For several years the Chautauquas were held on the grounds of the old Capitol, then the annual event was moved to the Second Street School. Long-time residents can recall the Lincoln Chautauqua coming every year and pitching tents on the schoolyard. This group portrait was made circa 1913. Photograph courtesy of Kentucky Historical Society.

The Institute for the Feeble-Minded was established on the outskirts of Frankfort in 1860. This 1911 view shows neatly dressed inmates in cooking class. The building was replaced by a modern structure that houses the Department of Human Resources. Postcard from the Sprague Postcard Collection. Photograph by Gretter; courtesy of Kentucky Historical Society.

The execution of Roger Warren on May 7, 1911, was the last hanging in Franklin County. Warren, a black convict at the Penitentiary, was sentenced to death for cutting the throat of another prisoner. A new law instituted electrocution. Photograph courtesy of Kentucky Historical Society.

The "Ladies Parlor" of the Frankfort Hotel in 1911. Photograph by Gretter; courtesy of Kentucky Historical Society.

J. J. King hired Frankfort artist Paul Sawyier to paint the murals in the hotel dining room. King, one of Sawyier's chief patrons, was described by Mary Hamel in the catalogue to the exhibition *a Kentucky Artist, Paul Sawyier* (1865-1917) as: "a non-practicing graduate engineer, who was independently wealthy, who traveled on safari, was an amateur photographer and filmmaker, and had an active appreciation for the arts." Photograph by Gretter; courtesy of Kentucky Historical Society.

Periodic temperance campaigns were held in Frankfort, but with twenty-four saloons in town in 1891, the battle was an uphill one. John C. Fuss tells the story of a time that William Jennings Bryan came to town to give a temperance lecture at the Opera House. A young man was sent next door to the Frankfort Hotel Bar for a pitcher of iced water for the speaker. The bartender, unimpressed with the purpose of the speech, slipped a "shoofly" in the water, forcing the great orator to end his speech prematurely. This is the Frankfort Hotel Bar in 1911. Photograph by Gretter; courtesy of Kentucky Historical Society.

Weehawken, circa 1915. The Trabue family purchased the estate with its frame building in 1839. When the frame house burned in 1860, Stephen Fitz-James Trabue had the present structure built. After his death in 1898, the mansion was sold to Stephen French Hoge, treasurer of the Hoge-Montgomery Company, a shoe factory. The building is now surrounded by the Bel Air subdivision. Photograph courtesy of Kentucky Historical Society.

The employees of Labrot & Graham posed for this shot in 1883. Photograph courtesy of Kentucky Library, Western Kentucky University.

Frankfort area distillers have been active from the beginning. One, the Capitol Brewery, was located near the head of Ann Street. That building became the Frankfort Brewery, and then a varnish factory. More typically, distilleries were built outside the city limits, often on the banks of the Kentucky River. This view of the E. H. Taylor Distillery dates from the late nineteenth century. Photograph courtesy of Kentucky Historical Society.

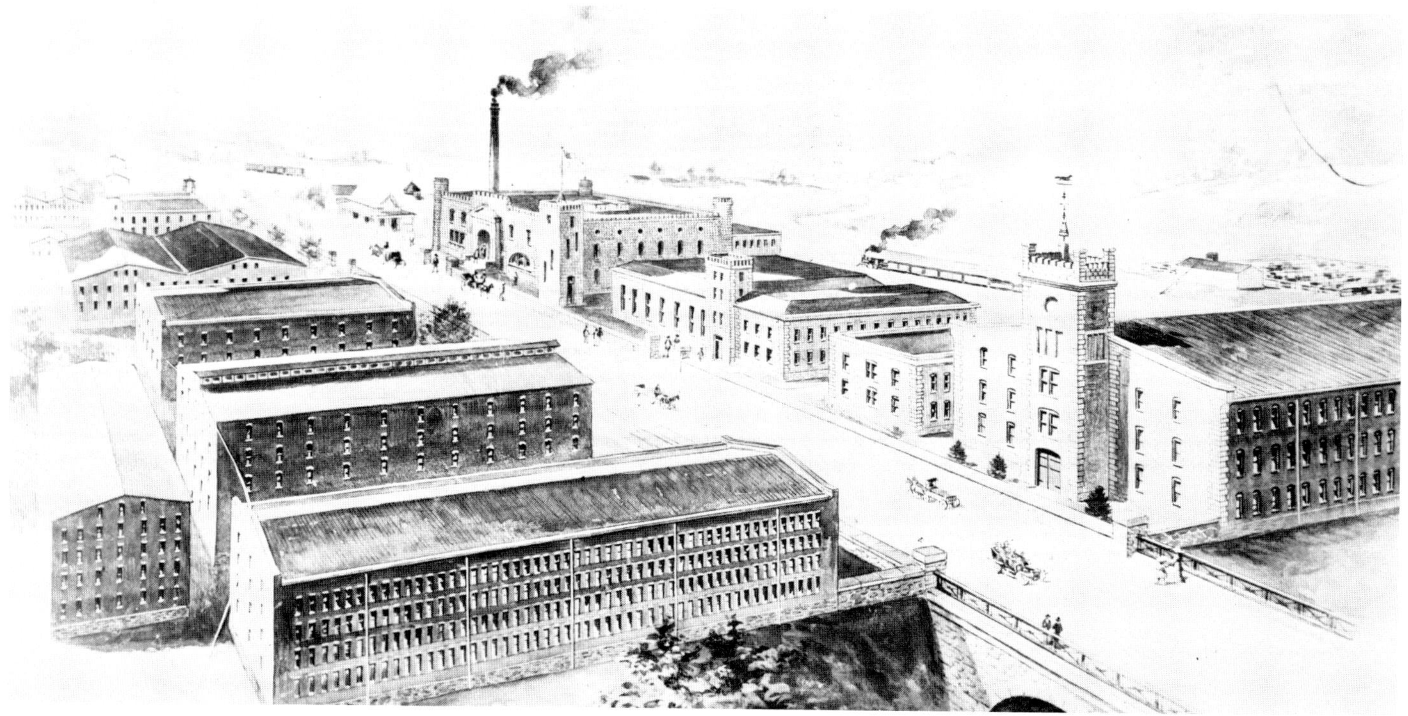

This panorama from the 1880s shows Hermitage Distillery. The 1881 Franklin County *Atlas* lists: "Hiram Berry of the firm of W. A. Gaines & Co., Proprietors of 'Hermitage' and 'Old Crow' Distilleries. Manufacturers of the celebrated brands of 'Hermitage'and 'Old Crow' whiskies." C. C. Furr was listed as clerk at Hermitage Distillery No. 4. Photograph courtesy of Kentucky Historical Society.

A photograph from the east side of the river shows Hermitage Distillery and the new Capitol. Courtesy of Kentucky Historical Society.

THE FRANKFORT MODES GLASS WORKS

INCORPORATED

FRANKFORT, KENTUCKY

MANUFACTURERS OF BOTTLES

FINEST WORKMANSHIP—PROMPT SERVICE

Flint and Amber Bottles for Distillery Bottling a Specialty

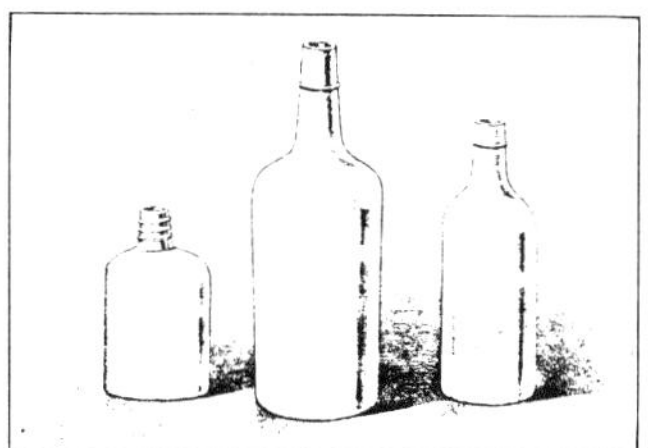

In Cartons and Printed Cases, Boxed or Crated as Desired

CAPACITY 180,000 GROSS PER ANNUM—ABOUT 725 CAR LOADS

GIVING EMPLOYMENT TO 450 MEN

FRANKFORT'S LARGEST SINGLE ENTERPRISE

GEO. B. HARPER, President — W. M. CULTER, Jr., Secretary — F. J. ARBOGAST, Superintendent

Because distilling requires bottling, it is not surprising that a glass works industry grew up in Frankfort. Advertisement courtesy of Kentucky Historical Society.

Boys playing football on the lawn of Berry Hill at the turn of the century. Built by George F. Berry, Secretary and Treasurer of W. A. Gaines and Company, Distillers, Berry Hill now houses the State Library. Photograph by Wolff; courtesy of Kentucky Historical Society.

The gothic revival music room at Berry Hill. Photograph courtesy of Kentucky Historical Society.

Thistleton, the elegant Queen Anne residence of E. H. Taylor, Jr., distillery owner and Frankfort mayor, was torn down in the early 1960s. The location on Louisville Road is now occupied by a motel and an apartment complex bearing the name of Taylor's estate. Photograph by Gretter; courtesy of Kentucky Historical Society.

The dining room at Thistleton as it appeared circa 1910. E. H. Taylor's portrait hangs on the wall. Photograph by Gretter; courtesy of Kentucky Historical Society.

This interior shot of the Old Taylor bottling plant is postmarked 1915. The bottles are similar to those made by the Frankfort Modes Glass Works. Courtesy of University of Kentucky Postcard Collection.

Old Taylor Distillery. Old Taylor is now part of National Distillers Products Company, who also run Old Crow and Old Grand Dad. Courtesy of Kentucky Historical Society.

October 1943, an Old Taylor milestone—the one-millionth case. Photograph courtesy of Kentucky Historical Society.

City Judge William C. Herndon in 1913. Photograph by Gretter; courtesy of Kentucky Historical Society.

An interior view of the Franklin County Court House in late 1910. The Court House is still in use. Photograph by Gretter; courtesy of Kentucky Historical Society.

James B. McCreary, governor from 1911 to 1915, poses with his driver in a new touring car. Photograph by Gretter; courtesy of Kentucky Historical Society.

The New Palace Saloon at 322 St. Clair Street is decorated for the inauguration of Governor McCreary in 1911. Coleman and McKeever's popular establishment was reputed to have a "friendly game" upstairs. M. Bertha Watson's millinery shop is next door. Photograph by Gretter; courtesy of Kentucky Historical Society.

In 1911 O. N. Smith and Company, 324-26 Ann Street, was a well-known wholesale grocer. In addition, the firm served as agents for the Moerlein Brewing Company and as proprietors of the Eagle Bottling Company. Photograph courtesy of Kentucky Historical Society.

As the seat of state government, Frankfort has always recognized the need for up-to-date snow removal equipment. The 1917 model snow plow is shown near the Post Office. Photograph by Gretter; courtesy of Kentucky Historical Society.

The *Courier-Journal's* Autocar made daily deliveries to Frankfort in 1911. During its glory years, the Louisville *Journal*, which was hyphenated in an 1868 merger, carried tremendous political clout. Photograph courtesy of Kentucky Historical Society.

As early as 1891 Dr. S. F. Smith of Frankfort was editor and owner of *The Witness*, a newspaper devoted to Woman Suffrage. In 1913 the editor of the *State Journal* would write: "Franklin County's suffragettes are not brick-throwing, screaming 'militants.' They are dimpled persuasives. Not one dollar of our hard-earned and elusive cash is going to bet against the success of the suffragettes." Advertisement courtesy of Kentucky Historical Society.

THE WITNESS.

THE WITNESS is devoted to Woman Suffrage and to the Promotion of Purity in Politics. It is the oldest and largest Reform paper published in the State. In fact it is the best family WEEKLY newspaper published in Kentucky.

It is the People's paper, the advocate of a government of the people, by the people and for the people.

SUBSCRIPTION RATES:

Twelve weeks, in advance, - - - -	$0.25
Six months, in advance, - - - -	.50
One year, in advance, - - - - -	1.00

Address,

THE WITNESS,

Box 302. FRANKFORT, KY.

EDDIE POLO in The
of the Circu
EDDIE POLO
HERCULES OF THE FILMS
UNIVERSAL
Greatest Film
Show on earth
HERE EVERY WEEK
NIEL BOONE
TRAIL
MOTION PICTURES
DANIEL B ONE ON THE TRA
POLO
CIRCUS
TODAY

The Daniel Boone Troupe came to town in 1919. They played at the Grand Theatre, 310 St. Clair Street, next to Woolworth's. Admission: fifteen cents for adults, ten cents for children. Photograph by Gretter; courtesy of Kentucky Historical Society.

Mary Swigert Hendricks poses for her photograph at The Terraces before her marriage to Edgar E. Hume. Photograph by Gretter; courtesy of Kentucky Historical Society.

The Service Motor Company, 315-17 West Second Street, pumped that "Good Gulf" gasoline. Shown in 1919, it first appears in the 1917-19 city directory. Later it became the Rowland Gooch auto repair shop and later still the Buick-Pontiac Company. The building was razed to make way for the Municipal Building. Photograph courtesy of Kentucky Historical Society.

The rear of J. Buford Hendrick's house, The Terraces, at 319 Wapping Street, shown here about 1905, was originally the main entrance. When Philip Swigert, an owner of steamboat interests, built the Greek Revival mansion in 1848, he faced it toward the river. The Terrances, torn down in 1954, was located where the city parking lot is today. Photograph by Gretter; courtesy of Kentucky Historical Society.

First Meeting

Frankfort Monday Music Club

Episcopal Parish House, November 5, 1923

OFFICERS OF CLUB

MRS. J. O. ROBERTS, *President.*

MISS STELLA SHAW, *Vice-President.*

MISS JOSEPHINE STRASSNER, *Secretary.*

MRS. OVERTON PARRENT, *Treasurer.*

MISS WILLANNA SMITH, *Chr. Press Com.*

MRS. CHAS. IRION, *Chr. Membership Com.*

MISS LUCY MARKHAM CHINN, *Chr. Program Com.*

MRS. FRANK HEWITT, *Historian.*

Music was not limited to the orchestra. The women of the Episcopal Church formed their own group in 1923. Program courtesy of Kentucky Historical Society.

Frankfort Orchestra, circa 1919. This popular dance band played throughout Kentucky. *Left to right, back row*: Van Winkler, John Ries, Claude Bowles, Eugene Triplett, Willard Winters, John Brady; *front row*: Winifred Brady, Archie Smither, Charles Ahler, Frank Gobber. Photograph courtesy of Kentucky Historical Society.

Ebner's soda fountain, 312 West Main Street, was a favorite gathering place for young people. This is the way it appeared, circa 1915. Photograph by Gretter; courtesy of Kentucky Historical Society.

Soda Water, Hot or Cold. Only the Juice of Fresh Fruit Used. Ice Cream of the Purest
Phone 23. 312 Main Street

Ebner & Co.

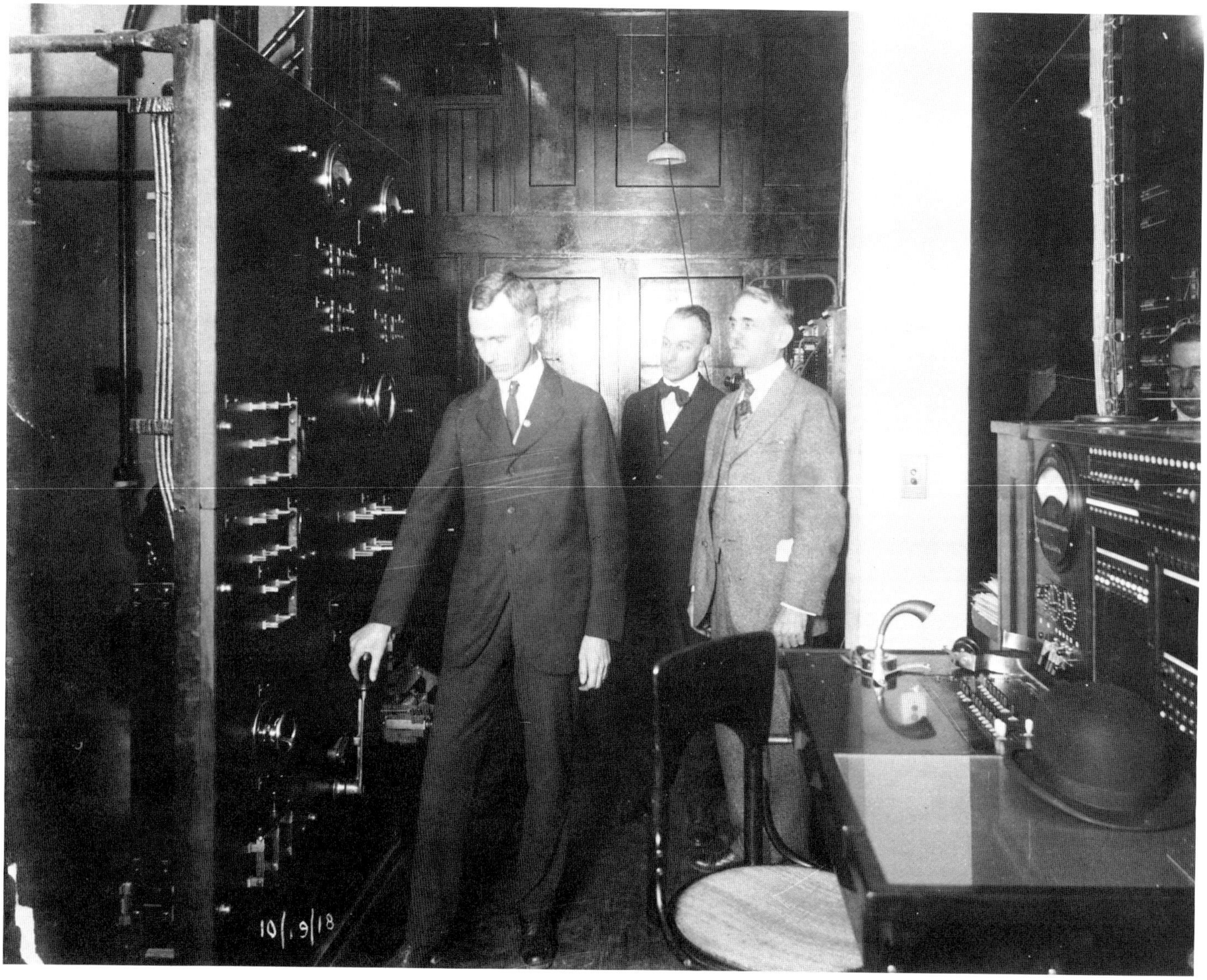

Cumberland Telephone Company, 1918. Frankfort had telephone service ever since about 1880, when M. H. P. Williams, Jr., Wiley Williams, and John William opened an exchange. An 1896 state business directory lists Frankfort's company as the East Tennessee Telephone Company, which became, by 1912, the Frankfort Telephone Company. A rival, the Frankfort Telephone Company (also known as the Home Telephone Company or Frankfort Home Telephone and Telegraph Company), was established in October 1899. The two rivals lasted into the 1920s. The South Central Bell Telephone Company presently serves the area. Photograph by Gretter; courtesy of Kentucky Historical Society.

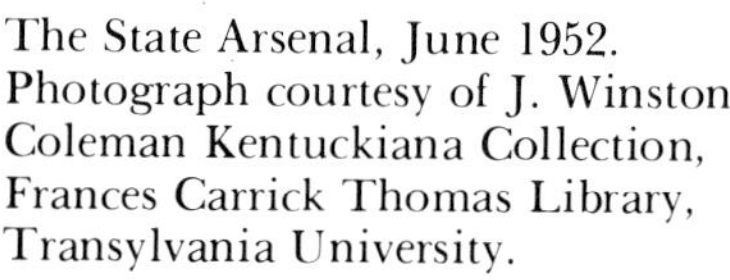

The State Arsenal, June 1952. Photograph courtesy of J. Winston Coleman Kentuckiana Collection, Frances Carrick Thomas Library, Transylvania University.

An 1850 legislative act authorized construction of the State Arsenal "for preservation of public arms." After having served the Kentucky Militia and National Guard since that date, the Arsenal became the Kentucky Military History Museum. This picture was taken in 1915. Photograph courtesy of Kentucky Military History Museum.

Workmen load supplies at the Arsenal for the Mexican Border expedition in 1916. Photograph courtesy of Kentucky Historical Society.

Julius Richer was named "Official Bugler of Franklin County" and played at special events during World War I. In this photograph he is performing near the military monument in the cemetery. Photograph courtesy of Kentucky Historical Society.

World War I

Postcard sized fact sheet bringing attention to Franklin County's generous response to her country's call, circa 1918. Courtesy of Kentucky Historical Society.

What Franklin County,

Kentucky, Has Done

Gave so many volunteers to the country that only four men were drafted.

Gave fifty boys to the Navy, who didn't count in reducing the quota for Military Service.

Had more contributors to the Red Cross War Fund in proportion to population than any other county.

Over-subscribed the first Liberty Loan $67,000 without a canvass.

Over-subscribed the second Liberty Loan $250,300, two and a quarter times as much as was subscribed the first time, nearly two and a quarter times the minimum allotment.

Is ready for any other call by the country upon her enthusiasm, efficiency, resources or patriotism.

Franklin gave her heart when she gave her sons; what she has left goes with them.

From a letter to the *Cincinnati Enquirer*, November 17, 1918: "Secretary Ben Marshall of the State Tax Commission this week gave further evidence that he is a political fighter who never misses an opportunity to land a blow. It will be recalled that Marshall was removed as Collector of Internal Revenue for the 7th District to make a place for General Percy Haly. Marshall's removal was accomplished only after Senator J. C. W. Beckham had stated that he was personally obnoxious to him. Now Marshall is circulating thousands of Post Cards upon which appear the likeness of himself and five boys in the service.... Marshall was succeeded as Collector in times of war by a very 'famous General' who had no troops to lead nor sons to give." Postcard courtesy of Kentucky Historical Society.

Turn of the century photograph of the Marshall family before the boys grew up to be soldiers. Photograph by Wolff; courtesy of Kentucky Historical Society.

A parade displayed Frankfort's support for the war effort. Photograph by Gretter; courtesy of Kentucky Historical Society.

Gretter photographed each group as it passed under his window. Across the street is a patriotic billboard: "Food will win the war. Don't waste it." Photograph courtesy of Kentucky Historical Society.

Flag-bearing doughboys lead a 1917 parade onto Main Street. The ruins of the Capitol Hotel appear at left. Photograph courtesy of Kentucky Historical Society.

Many Americans felt that modernism and internationalism were destroying the American way of life. Congress had passed laws limiting immigration; prohibition had become law; anti-evolutionist battles had been fought in Kentucky and Tennessee. The Ku Klux Klan, though remembered mainly for its anti-Jewish and anti-black biases, stressed the old values. This circa 1925 photographs shows a Klan funeral. Courtesy of Kentucky Historical Society.

The Capital Theatre was used for many purposes, including live entertainment and movies. The Elks used the facilities for a 1926 memorial service. At the turn of the century people often called it the Opera House. Program courtesy of Kentucky Historical Society.

Our Honored Dead

William H. Stone
Lee H. Cohen
William Frances Barrett
Micheal Buckley
John T. Gray
William R. Magoffin
John Bradley
Joseph C. Thomas
Owen M. Furr
John B. Dryden
Alfred M. Slack
Walter G. Chapman
L. M. Sanford
Thomas C. Jones
William Lindsay
D. Howard Johnson
Julian Tilford
James R. Thompson
James R. Ely
Pat J. O'Brien
Lafe Wells
C. E. Cromwell
Joseph Swigert
James H. Graham
John H. Stuart, P.E.R.
L. C. Briant
George Baker
H. B. H. Klosterman
Albert W. Mowbray
Frank Heeney
William P. Hudson
W J. Baker
T. Hiter Crockett
Archie W. Smither
John A. Brislan
Thomas A. Hall
James R. Shaw
A. Z. Churchill
D. W. Lindsey
James S. Deshon
L. F. Webb, Jr.
James F. Montgomery
Louis H. Weitzel
John S. Cannon
Thomas J. Brislan
Fred W. Johnson
Sam M. Lykins
Henry Ringold
John F. Dolan
Fred W. Jones
Stephen Black
Franklin V. Gray
Paul C. Gaines
Robert A. Brawner
Robert Rhodes Settle
Preston L. Gibson
C. E. Collins
Don R. Todd
E. H. Taylor, Jr.
D. P. Richardson
James McAuliffe
S. M. Noel
James H. Hazelrigg
W. H. Posey
Henry J. Harris
George W. Parker
George W. Johnson
T. McClure Pythian
C. O. Reynolds, P.E.R.
Geo. C. Shaw

"The faults of our brothers we write upon the sands, their virtues upon the tablets of love and memory"

Memorial Services
Frankfort Lodge No. 530
Capital Theatre, December 5th, 1926

Opening Ceremonies .... By the Officers

Invocation .... Chaplain Jas. H. Polsgrove

Song--"Onward Christian Soldiers" .... Elks and Audience

Ceremonies .... By the Officers

Quartet--"My Soul Doth Magnify the Lord" .. C. B. Hawley

Ceremonies .... By the Officers

Duet--"The Lord is My Light" .... Dudley Buck
Mrs. Geo. M. Gayle and Orton S. Clark

Address .... Bro. W. T. Fowler

Quartet--"God Shall Wipe Away All Tears" .... L. H. Mills

Quartette--
Orton S. Clark
Mrs. Geo. W. Gayle
Mrs. Chas. Irion
Richard McClure

Benediction .... Chaplain Jas. H. Polsgrove

Accompanist .... Chas. R. Clayton

Music Director .... Bro. J. W. Ireland

Instrumental Music .... Gobber-Triplett Orchestra

Looking north on St. Clair Street in 1925. Photograph by Cusick; courtesy of Kentucky Historical Society.

Cusick's photograph was retouched—the wires and horse and buggy removed—and made into a postcard. Courtesy of University of Kentucky Postcard Collection.

Christmas lights in 1930 give Frankfort that "big city" look. Photograph by Cusick; courtesy of Kentucky Historical Society.

This daylight view in the twenties was taken from the same spot. Photograph by Cusick; courtesy of Kentucky Historical Society.

The mounting of a captured German howitzer in front of the old Capitol showed Frankfort's pride in its role in "the war to end all wars." This gun was melted down during a World War II scrap drive. This view is noteworthy, for the two historic structures parallel to the cannon have since been razed. The corner Madison-Harlan house was built by Kentucky Governor George Madison, who took office and died in 1816. Later it became the residence of Supreme Court Justice John Marshall Harlan, who served between 1877 and 1911. To the right is the Solomon P. Sharp house, where Jereboam O. Beauchamp assassinated the owner in 1825. The Capital Plaza complex extends to the street on which these two buildings fronted. Photograph by Cusick; courtesy of Kentucky Historical Society.

Church of the Ascension possibly at Christmas 1930. *Right to left*: Chick Hulette, crucifer; Sally Page Mason; Anne Brown, organist; Elizabeth Taylor Vansant; unknown; Genevieve Gayle; unknown; Mary Louise McGowan. The next six are unidentified and followed by: Mrs. W. H. Kidd, Stella Shaw, Mary Elizabeth Turner (Baker), Clem O'Connor, Ben M. Keenon, Thomas Knight, Bosworth M. Todd, Chester Watson, Major T. W. Woodyard, Billy Clayton, Richard McClure, Paul Meagher, and the Reverend E. W. Baxter. Photograph courtesy of Kentucky Historical Society.

On July 4, 1928, in Frankfort Cemetery, the Kentucky chapters of the Daughters of the American Revolution unveiled a monument to the Revolutionary War soldiers buried in Kentucky. Photograph courtesy of Kentucky Historical Society.

"Welcome Lafoon" banners deck Capital Avenue for his inauguration as governor in 1931. Ruby Lafoon was welcomed to a "salary of $6,500 per year and use of the mansion, but nothing furnished," according to *Caron's City Directory* for that year. Photograph by Cusick; courtesy of Kentucky Historical Society.

The Jazz Age swept through town in 1930 under the leadership of Morris Scott, *standing*, and his Jazz Hounds. Photograph by Cusick; courtesy of Kentucky Historical Society.

Sower's Hardware, 217-219 St. Clair Street, makes the hard sell in 1930 with the evidence of what a Hoover could pick up in just *one* Frankfort home. The founder, Pete Sower, was the grandfather of Frank Sower, Frankfort's former mayor and great-grandfather of present mayor John Sower. Photograph by Cusick; courtesy of Kentucky Historical Society.

A luscious assortment of Rebecca-Ruth candy as it was packaged in 1930. This famous Frankfort company, located at 104 West Second Street, was founded by Ruth Hanly Booe and Rebecca B. Gooch, the latter withdrawing from the business in 1929. Most famous for their Bourbon-flavored candy, the company still produces a wide range of confections. Photograph by Cusick; courtesy of Kentucky Historical Society.

A crowd of shoppers takes advantage of a sale at Newberry's in 1931. Photograph by Cusick; courtesy of Kentucky Historical Society.

J.J. NEWBERRY CO.
1.19
$1.00
25¢
J.J. NEWBERRY CO.
BOYS
TENNIS SHOES
89¢
10¢
10¢

Annie Laurie Cusick, who is sitting in the front row above the words "5th year," invited a few friends to celebrate her birthday, August 25, 1930. Photograph courtesy of Kentucky Historical Society.

An aerial view of Frankfort in the flood year 1937, when the city was surrounded by wide open spaces. Compare it with the 1978 flood photograph. Courtesy of National Archives, Center for Cartographic and Architectural Archives.

Kentucky State Industrial College May Queen, 1935. Photograph courtesy of Kentucky Historical Society.

Kiwanis Club Christmas party for orphans, 1939. Photograph courtesy of Kentucky Historical Society.

HOWSER'S
LUNCH

Flood of 1937

The flood of late January 1937 eclipsed all previous records. The 1883 flood had crested at 42.8 feet and the one of 1913 at 38 feet. The 1937 flood surpassed the old marks, peaking at 47.6 feet. Though the 1978 flood's 49.8-foot crest was higher still, the impact was greater in the thirties. The almost imperceptible hump between the St. Clair Street Bridge and the old Capitol was breeched in 1937, but not in 1978. Thus we have the spectacular view of St. Clair Street in 1937.

Likewise there was high drama when the water lapped around the Penitentiary and the convicts were transferred to second-story cells. Frightened convicts reacted in different ways; some rioting took place between blacks and whites; some convicts attempted to escape by jumping into the icy waters that swirled around the prison. With nearly three thousand prisoners in the antiquated facility, area residents became understandably uneasy. The situation eased as the governor pardoned several hundred lesser offenders and sent many of the remainder to the grounds of the Feeble-Minded Institute, to jails in Lexington, and elsewhere. The flood accomplished what reformers were unable to do as the prison was closed and replaced by the Eddyville facility.

St. Clair Street. Photograph courtesy of Kentucky Historical Society.

The Penitentiary walls crumble. Photograph courtesy of Kentucky Historical Society.

Boating on Capitol Avenue. Photograph courtesy of Kentucky Historical Society.

Main Street, circa 1945. The stone house, *left foreground*, was built in 1840 by John Hampton, and became a boarding house for lumberjacks who rafted logs from the upper reaches of the Kentucky River to the sawmills at the river's edge. The stone house remains a boarding house. The interurban station was located approximately where the Gulf sign appears. Photograph by Hill; courtesy of Kentucky Historical Society.

The Kentucky River, circa 1945. Frankfort residents recall that the river has frozen many times in this century, affording the opportunity for ice skating and other winter sports. Photographs courtesy of Kentucky Historical Society.

Main Street during World War II. *Tars and Spars* is playing at the Capital Theatre. Photograph by Cline of Chattanooga; courtesy of University of Kentucky Postcard Collection.

Noonan's, 200 West Second Street, in 1940. Photograph by Hill; courtesy of Kentucky Historical Society.

You'll Always Find

AT NOONAN'S

Because nothing but the best is ever considered for this store's shelves. Due to wartime conditions we were unable to furnish our customers with many of the fine foods it was our custom to stock, but before long we expect to have many of them back again. Some are returning now, and most every day we welcome back an item that was popular with our customers in pre-war days.

S&W
LARGE WHOLE
Peeled Apricots
S&W

Eager shoppers inspect the new home of Fitzgerald's Drugs, 229 West Main Street, in 1941. Photograph by Hill; courtesy of Kentucky Historical Society.

SURGICAL DRESSINGS
PRODUCTS MONTH
ORLIS DENTAL SPECIAL
29¢

W. T. GAINES & SON,

LIVERY,

FEED & SALE STABLE.

Saddle Horses and Vehicles for Hire. Rates to Commercial Men. Horses Boarded by Day or Month. Telephone No. 18.

CORNER CLINTON AND ST. CLAIR STS., REAR OF CAPITOL BUILDING, } Frankfort, Ky.

Buildings in Frankfort have seen multiple uses. Gaines and Son Livery appears in this 1940 photograph as the Model Laundry. The building is still in use as a storage facility. Photograph by Hill; courtesy of Kentucky Historical Society.

Frankfort residents will recognize this corner, 330 Ann Street, which in 1940 housed the Greyhound Bus Station, as the home of another familiar landmark—Putt's Restaurant. Photograph by Hill; courtesy of Kentucky Historical Society.

Vaughan's Garage on Second Street, 1941. The large residential building is, in 1980, the Rogers Funeral Home. The two service station buildings remain. Photograph courtesy of Kentucky Historical Society.

dreft
dreft
dreft

Lutkemeier's store was founded in 1862 and remained in operation for nearly a century. The founder's grandson Joe was quoted by Ermina Jett Darnell in her *Filling the Chinks*: "A store looking too tidy is one that is not doing much business." Photograph by Hill; courtesy of Kentucky Historical Society.

Mayor Coleman kicks off Frankfort's war bonds sale in 1942. *Left to right*: Cordelia Mefford, unknown, Mayor Coleman, Louise Sullivan Hanrahan. Photograph courtesy of Kentucky Historical Society.

World War II

Franklin County Draft Board inducting the first volunteers, 1940. Photograph courtesy of Kentucky Historical Society.

Radio station WFKY studio in 1945 in its pristine state. The station officially started operation in February 1946. In November 1977 another Frankfort station, WKED, went on the air. Photograph courtesy of Kentucky Historical Society.

Opposite Top:
Nurses' Aid class in 1943. Photograph courtesy of Kentucky Historical Society.

Opposite Bottom:
Armored vehicles parade down Capital Avenue shortly after the end of World War II. Photograph by Hill; courtesy of Kentucky Historical Society.

Armor crewmen prepare to mount up for a postwar parade. Photograph by Hill; courtesy of Kentucky Historical Society.

Frankfort High School, April 1979. Photograph by Stuart Sprague.

Frankfort High School football squad on Panther Day, 1947. Photograph courtesy of Kentucky Historical Society.

Peacetime saw the remodeling of the Midland Tavern in 1946. Photograph by Hill; courtesy of Kentucky Historical Society.

This property at 320 Ann Street housed J. B. Scott Livery in 1912, with C. D. Seay, veterinarian, attending. With the coming of the automobile as an article of common usage, the property was by 1921 converted to the Nicol Garage, dealers in Reos, Olds, and Chevrolets. Sometime in the period between 1922 and 1937, the building became Packard and Nash Sales and Service. This 1947-48 view shows Peden Motors with its new crop of post-war Ford trucks. By 1973 the property became the Capitol Parking Lot. Photograph by Hill; courtesy of Kentucky Historical Society.

In 1948 the Capital Shoe Shine at 234 St. Clair Street was a good place to swap sports stories. City directories indicate that as early as 1914 George Dagres and Thomas Darves operated an establishment under this name at this location. In the early twenties Christopher Steffos was listed as the owner. For a span of at least fifteen years, 1926-40, Harry Pappadimitropoulos was the proprietor. Theodore K. Demerson was the owner at the time of this photograph; from the calendar on the wall, the old regulator clock, and the baseball results, it can be determined that the photograph was taken at 4:33 P.M., Saturday, May 8, 1948. Sports talk that day probably centered around the A's ripping the Chisox and pulling off the season's first triple play as well as the lowly St. Louis Browns upset win over the Red Sox. The building now houses the Morris Realty and Auction Company. Photograph by Hill; courtesy of Kentucky Historical Society.

Red Yancey's was a popular restaurant on St. Clair Street. This view was taken in 1948. Photograph by Hill; courtesy of Kentucky Historical Society.

The State National Bank staff in 1951: *Left to right*: unknown, Stanley Berry, Sr., Miss Cotton, unknown, Charles E. Hoge, Ralph Callahan, Wellington Matthews, unknown, unknown, and Miss Black. Photograph by Hill; courtesy of Kentucky Historical Society.

J. Forrest Cusick bought Gretter's photographic studio in 1920. In the mid-thirties, after Cusick's death, the studio at 105½ St. Clair Street continued under the ownership of his widow Anna, with George A. Hill as photographer. After the war Joseph F. Hill, a brother, became photographer until the studio closed in 1958. This view of Cusick's studio, taken in the 1950s, is memorable for several generagions of Frankfort residents. Photograph by Hill; courtesy of Kentucky Historical Society.

Courtesy of J. Winston Coleman Collection of Kentuckiana, Frances Garrick Thomas Library, Transylvania University.

The J. Winston Coleman photograph of St. Clair Street in 1951 contrasts dramatically with the April 1979 view, for in 1974 a mall was constructed and lanterns were added.

Photograph by Stuart Sprague.

Opposite Left:
The New Capital Hotel became the State National Bank—another outstanding example of creative recycling of important landmarks. Photograph by Stuart Sprague, April 1979.

8027
L&N
8027
FAMILY LINES SYSTEM

Modern Frankfort

Photograph by Stuart Sprague, April 1979

These views, the first two taken from opposite ends of the St. Clair Street Bridge, symbolize the evolutions of the past twenty years. The bridge has just received a new coat of paint and the old YMCA has been preserved as a governmental office building housing, among other units, the Kentucky Heritage Commission. On the other hand, a dump truck awaits a fresh load of rubble as wreckers work on a corner building.

Continuity and change, preservation and demolition are at work. L & N engines 8027 and 1539 pull a string of freight cars, disrupting traffic wishing to cross Broadway as trains have for more than a century and a quarter. The Farmers Bank Building is anything but traditional in its style or bulk, and yet the clock in front of the building ties the financial institution to its past.

The interstate highway system and network of access roads have pulled business away from the downtown area. Miracle miles with fast food chains and scattered plazas/shopping centers have developed. Meanwhile the number of year-round state workers has increased. This has led to periods of urban renewal: demolition and preservation.

The Craw, the black ghetto that also was the scene of a colorful and sometimes crime-ridden night life—with the Blue Moon, Peach Tree Inn, The Rendezvous, Sky Blue Inn, Tiger Inn, and Tip Toe Inn—is no more; the Capital Plaza Complex replaces it.

The head of the Urban Renewal Commission in late 1963 declared that the downtown began to decline in the late 1940s, that "the downtown is characterized by obsolescence, deteriorated buildings, apathetic property owners, traffic congestion, and parking problems. Most property has been in the same hands for fifty years or longer and is tied up in estates with infant heirs or held by absentee landlords who have little regard for property conditions and appearance, and attend only to collect rents or seek lower tax rates. Pride in their city is not a word in their vocabulary."

As in the nation as whole, a backlash developed. Property owners and public-minded citizens alike woke up to the fact that a priceless heritage was being destroyed. One of Frankfort's answers was the St. Clair Street Mall. Likewise, the constantly increasing cost of new construction made the creative recycling of old landmarks an economically advantageous alternative to building from scratch. In the case of older structures that because of shape or function are not easily converted, they are often razed and replaced by parking lots.

Kentucky Air National Guard jets salute Governor Breathitt at his inauguration ceremony in 1964. Photograph courtesy of Kentucky Historical Society.

New construction of state buildings has been usual in the years since World War II, as illustrated by the May 1953 view of the Capitol annex. Photograph courtesy of J. Winston Coleman Kentuckiana Collection, Frances Carrick Thomas Library, Transylvania University.

Many readers will remember when the old Capitol was the home of the Kentucky Historical Society. The cramped quarters housed all the relics now on display in the new quarters of the Kentucky Historical Society and the Military Museum at the State Arsenal. Photograph courtesy of University of Kentucky, Department of Interior Collection.

The Frank Lloyd Wright House at 509 Shelby Street, the only Wright-designed building in Kentucky, was built for the Reverend Jesse R. Zeigler, a young Presbyterian minister. Wright and Zeigler met on an ocean voyage during the summer of 1910. The architect continued on to Italy and sent sketches back to his Oak Park workshop, where the firm drew up blue prints. Zeigler occupied the house for five years, Mr. and Mrs. James Owen Roberts for ten years, and various tenants for two decades; in 1948 the present owner, Mrs. W. C. Weitzel, purchased the building. Frank Lloyd Wright did not see the structure until 1948, when he delivered a lecture at the University of Louisville. Photograph by Stuart Sprague, November 1978.

The St. Clair Street Bridge is given a fresh undercoating in this April 1979 photograph. By May a fresh blue overcoat was added. Notice the painters with their buckets in the superstructure and the tower of the Capitol Plaza Complex rising in the background. Photograph by Stuard Sprague.

From at least the early 1880s until the 1950s the Frankfort Fire Department was awkwardly located on Main Street near St. Clair. Then the city acquired the Frankfort Buick-Pontiac Company's Second Street property and constructed the present municipal complex. Originally the John H. Hanna house stood on this site facing the St. Clair Street Bridge. Photograph by Stuart Sprague, April 1979.

Main Street from the old Farmers Bank (Teachers Retirement Office) to the old New Capitol Hotel (State National Bank). These two photographs were taken under the canopy of the facade of the Capitol Theatre at the height of the May 1979 Democratic primary. Note the Mills for Secretary of State Headquarters and the intriguing rooflines that are typical of the newly created Frankfort Commercial Historical District. Photograph by Stuart Sprague.

The Capital Theatre, January 1979. With residents and businesses moving to the suburbs and the malls—Eastwood Shopping Center, Winn-Dixie Shopping Center, Frankfort Plaza, Franklin Square Shopping Center, Brighton Park, and others—and with the strip development of the roads leading out of Frankfort, a downtown theatre was no longer economically sound. How different from the days of World War II when there were several theatres and new double features were brought in about twice a week! In the daytime, parking space brings a premium downtown. Nearly half the urban landmarks that have been razed in America have been destroyed to serve as parking lots. This is no exception. To see a movie in Frankfort today, one must go to Franklin Square or Brighton Park—two new shopping centers. Photograph by Stuart Sprague.

Through the years the view of the city from Frankfort Cemetery has intrigued photographers. The bulky building, *center*, is the Farmers Bank. Photograph by Stuart Sprague, April 1979.

The construction of Capital Plaza in the early seventies radically changed the face of the area known as Craw. The complex, designed by Edward Durell Stone, includes a state office tower, a federal building, a YMCA, a sports and convention center, and a shopping mall. Photograph courtesy of the Department of Public Information.

Louisville, Ky., Sunday morning, December 10, 1978 60¢

258 Pages
Vol. 247, No. 163
★★★★★

The Courier-Journal

Sunday
Home delivery:
55¢

Copyright © 1978, The Courier-Journal

Frankfort is hit by its worst flood since '37

December 1978. Courtesy of *The State Journal.*

Not only does this mosaic show the extent of the flood's damage, but can be compared with the 1937 aerial photograph. Note the improved roads and the increased area built up. Satellite flood photograph, December 12, 1978; courtesy of Kentucky Historical Society.

Bibliography

Atlas of Frankfort and Franklin County, Kentucky 1870-1880. Frankfort, Kentucky: Bur-Wal Association, 1971.

Averill, William H. *A History of the First Presbyterian Church, Frankfort, Kentucky Together with the Churches in Franklin County in Connection with the Presbyterian Church in the United States of America*. Frankfort, Kentucky: 1901.

Darnell, Ermina Jett *South Frankfort, Kentucky*. Frankfort, Kentucky: Roberts Printing Company, 1947.

Hitchcock, Henry-Russell and William Seale *Temples of Democracy: The State Capitols of the USA*. New York: Harcourt Brace Jovanich, 1976.

Jillson, Willard Rouse *Early Frankfort and Franklin County Kentucky: a Chronology of Historical Sketches Covering the Century 1750-1850*. Louisville: Standard Printing Co., 1936.

_________ *An Historical Bibliography of Frankfort, Kentucky 1751-1941*. Frankfort, Kentucky: State Journal Company, 1942.

Johnson, Lewis Franklin *History of Franklin County, Kentucky*. Frankfort: Roberts Publishing Company, 1921.

_________ *The History of Franklin County, Kentucky*. Frankfort, Kentucky: Roberts Printing Company, 1912.

Klotter, James Christopher *William Goebel: The Politics of Wrath*. Lexington, Kentucky: University Press of Kentucky, 1977.

Index

About the authors:

Stuart S. Sprague is presently professor of history at Morehead State University in Morehead, Kentucky. He holds a B.A. and M.A.T. from Yale University and a Ph.D. in history from New York University (1972), and worked as a research librarian for the American History, Local History and Genealogy Divisions of the New York Public Library before joining the faculty of Morehead in 1968. Professor Sprague is presently working on a book about the Appalachian region of Kentucky.

Elizabeth A. Perkins is curator of the Kentucky Historical Museum, a division of the the Kentucky Historical Society. She holds a B.S. is history from Centre College of Kentucky (1974), and has been with the museum since graduation, formerly as an assistant curator and curator of exhibits. She was project director for "An Interpretation of 19th Century Kentucky History," sponsored by the National Endowment for the Humanities, which produced eight museum exhibits on historical and cultural topics of Kentucky history.